The Abba FOUNDATION

Dr. Chiqui Wood
With Dr. Kerry Wood

Cover Design: Ivethe Zambrano-Fernández
wwwdesignbytwo.com

Photography of Author by John Choate

Bedford, Texas
www.BurkhartBooks.com

Dedication

It is with much gratitude that I dedicate this work to my friend,

Dr. Wess Pinkham.

Acknowledgments

I am so grateful to my husband, Kerry Wood, who personifies the other-centered, self-giving love of the Father, Son, and Holy Spirit. Kerry excels in the "competition of generosity" and I'm the happy recipient of his love and constant encouragement. Not only is Kerry a wonderful husband; but his teaching has added much depth to my understanding of spiritual matters. I've been privileged to sit under his teaching for years, and even more so to have the honor of partnering with him in ministry. We love teaching together; so much so, that at this point I honestly couldn't tell you if some of my thoughts originated with me or with him. So, wherever credit is due, thank you, Baby! On so many levels I can honestly say, "I couldn't have done it without you."

My gratitude also goes to Dr. Wess Pinkham. One of the best decisions I have ever made was participating in the Doctor of Ministry program under his direction. Dr. Wess, as his students call him, is one of those rare individuals who has multiple advanced degrees, and yet teaches by impartation of his own transformative journey since he was "ambushed by *Abba*." It was in one of Dr. Wess' classes that I became profoundly aware of the significance of Jesus' relationship with His *Abba*, and how when we look at Jesus, what we see is a Son whose eyes are set on His Father. It was while reading one of Dr. Wess' manuscripts that I heard a prompting by the Holy Spirit: "what if we could help people know the Father?" And so, my doctoral journey began—a journey of discovery, of personal transformation and growth, and most importantly, a journey of becoming keenly aware of the many *Abba* hugs we were receiving daily.

Dr. Wess introduced me to significant people, like Dr. Marty Folsom, who became my project mentor. Marty is one of those unique theologians that helps us connect the dots to see the practicality of sound Trinitarian theology. I am grateful for his prodding and encouragement to dig deeper and sharpen my theology.

Through the readings I came to know others, like Brennan Manning who can describe the Father's love in profound, yet simple ways; Ray Anderson, Karl Barth, Gordon Fee, Stanley Grenz, Colin Gunton, Jack Hayford, John Macmurray, Alistair McFadyen, J. B. Torrance, T. F. Torrance, Dallas Willard, and N. T. Wright, whose theology has shaped mine; and many others, who have contributed to this writing. I have tried to give credit where credit is due, so you will see them listed in the footnotes and bibliography.

My love for *Abba* has increased exponentially, and my hope is that this book will be my contribution for many others to come to know the *Abba* of Jesus, to be ambushed by His love, to feel at home in His presence, and to embark on a journey of discovery, awe and wonder in the love of our God.

I owe a great debt of gratitude to Donna Burley, Scharlotte Celestine, Cathy Haggard, Ryan Northcutt, Wess Pinkham, and Kerry Wood, my wonderful friends who took time to read the manuscripts and provide feedback, corrections, questions, and suggestions to help me communicate more clearly.

Thank you to Tod and Tammy Williams, for the use of their "Twelve Stones" cabin for our writing retreat, where most of these pages were composed.

Contents

Preface

Jesus' last instruction before ascending to the Father is commonly called the Great Commission: "Go therefore and make disciples of all nations" (Matthew 28:19). This often raises the question, "What is a disciple?" or "What does a true disciple of Jesus look like?"

To say that many books have been written on the subject would be an understatement. A simple online search on the topic returns over 10,000 book titles. Some of these have to do with a call to making disciples; others are biblical studies related to discipleship; but the vast majority propose practical steps that will result in discipleship. The general idea espoused in this literature is that we are saved by grace; but once we are born again, we must learn the disciplines, behaviors and attitudes of a Christian so we can grow into Christlikeness. But spiritual growth is the *result* of relationship with God, not the *cause* of it.

In fact, a preoccupation with behavior and performance often becomes an obstacle rather than an aid to our relationship with God. For example, pastors or leaders may want people to develop a discipline of prayer, thinking that prayer will enhance their relationship with God. However, as Henri Nouwen points out, most people live their lives in a context of fear—fear of others, fear of God, and anxiety in general. So, when they try to approach God in prayer, their fear drives them to the many distractions the world has to offer.[1] And who wants to pray if there is a subconscious idea that God is judgmental, perfectionistic, or angry? But they know they are supposed to pray! (That's what "good Christians" do). So, they feel like a failure in their prayer life, which only exacerbates the fear, which keeps them from developing the discipline of prayer. This vicious circle is what we often see when we emphasize behaviors and performance. As Ray Anderson says, "Too often we attempt to build our discipling programs on conformity to rules, disciplines, and control-minded religious personalities." These programs "can produce religious robots, who may lack the true motive for discipleship, which is love."

Moreover, the preoccupation with right behavior stands in opposition to the Gospel of grace. As Brennan Manning says:

Spiritual growth is the result of relationship with God, not the cause of it.

My definition of "disciple" is one who freely receives the Father's love and responds to His presence, evidenced by other-centered love and action. The American Church today accepts grace in theory but denies it in practice. We say we believe the fundamental structure of reality is grace, not works—but our lives refute our faith. By and large, the gospel of grace is neither proclaimed, understood, nor lived. Too many Christians are living in the house of fear and not in the house of love.[3]

What does living in the "house of fear" mean? Allow me to illustrate with a couple of examples. A friend was sharing her concern over making a wrong decision and explained, "I'm terrified of God's discipline." Her apprehension was genuine; but her reasoning revealed an unhealthy perspective of God. Sadly, she is not alone in this sentiment. Many Christians share this fear (and perhaps you are one of them). As part of my doctoral work I conducted surveys among Christians in four different settings between 2011 and 2014, and found that more than half of those surveyed live in fear of God's discipline; 82% of them believe that God is repulsed by sin; and 67% believe that no matter how hard they try, they don't quite measure up to the holiness that God expects from them.[4] They are living in the "house of fear."

A pastor recently asked his congregation, "How many of you think God can't look at you except through Christ because of how awful you are?" Not surprisingly, many raised their hands. They, too, are living in the "house of fear." Reflecting on this response he observes, "I think our wrong thinking about God is at the core of much that goes wrong in the Church and the world … If we start from a place of thinking God is angry with us, then no matter how much He shows His love we are going to drop back to a performance mindset."[5] At some point, we hold a love for God as an abstraction but live as though He is very distant. If He might be angry isn't it better that He is busy somewhere else?

The problem with discipleship in our context (the Western Church in the 21st century) is that we have been approaching it from the wrong angle. Something needs to change. I lean again on Brennan Manning who suggests a different approach:

We need a new kind of relationship with the Father that drives out fear and mistrust and anxiety and guilt, that permits us to be hopeful and joyous, trusting and compassionate. We have to be converted from the bad news to the good news, from expecting nothing to expecting something.[6]

I write this book from the conviction that disciples aren't made by focusing on behaviors, attitudes, or even the disciplines of a disciple; but by focusing on God instead. Based on this, my definition of "disciple" is *one who freely receives the Father's love and responds to His presence, evidenced by other-centered love and action.* Discipleship, then, is a process of transformation by God's indwelling presence (by the Holy Spirit), as we cultivate our relationship with God and with one another. In this process our beliefs, attitudes, and behaviors progressively reflect the image of Christ—as the fulfilled human in relationship with both God and neighbor. If this is the case, then we must ask, "How do we grow as disciples of Jesus?"

Jesus said the first and greatest commandment is to "love the Lord your God with all your heart and with all your soul and with all your mind" (Matthew 22:37); therefore, it seems self-evident that the foundation for discipleship should be experiencing God's love—His way of being—rather than focusing on principles and disciplines.

How did Jesus take twelve simple men and turn them into the most radical world-changers in history? A key is found in Mark's Gospel, where he says that Jesus "appointed twelve, that they might be with Him and that He might send them out to preach, and to have power to heal sicknesses and to cast out demons" (Mark 3:14-15). We often focus on the sending and doing part; but fail to notice that He first appointed them that they might be with Him. Jesus' approach to discipleship was grounded in relationship—a relationship of love and proximity—so it follows that if we want to be Christ-like, more than focusing on what we do, our priority should be setting our eyes on the Father; knowing the love of *Abba*; receiving His love, and knowing who we are in Him.

Disclaimer

Whole books could be written—and in fact, many have been written—on each of the subjects covered in this book. My goal is not

Our priority should be setting our eyes on the Father; knowing the love of Abba; receiving His love, and knowing who we are in Him.

to give a comprehensive treatment of each; nor to answer all possible questions on the matter. My desire is to give us a framework for knowing the Father, the *Abba* of Jesus, as Jesus reveals Him to be. My goal is to draw us closer to the heart of the Father, that we would have a revelation of His love that would allow us to lean into the mystery of the unknown—the unanswered questions—with the assurance that *Abba* is good; that *Abba* loves us, and that *Abba* can be trusted.

For those of you who want to delve deeper into the subjects I address, I have provided footnotes to point you to scholars who speak more thoroughly about these subjects. I am eternally indebted to each of these authors. Their writings have both inspired and challenged me. Their works have shaped my theology, and what you hold in your hand would be impossible without their work. We truly stand on the shoulders of giants, and I am grateful for the many men and women who have invested in my life.

My Desire for You

When I set out to write this book, I thought the task would be easy. Over the last ten years I have taught this series of lessons, in some form or another, multiple times. I am passionate about this theme. But when I teach them, I use visual illustrations, exercises, discussion questions, and activities that reinforce what we're saying. Putting all of this in book form is much harder than I anticipated.

My desire for you is that you get as much out of reading the book as others have gotten out of participating in the classes. So, my encouragement to you is that you invite a few friends to go on this journey with you. Read the book together, talk about it, discuss the questions on the back of each chapter, engage with the reflections and the prayers. My desire is that you will have an encounter with the Father, the *Abba* of Jesus, through each of the chapters in this book; and you will experience it more fully when you do it in relationship with others.

Introduction

When we look to Jesus, we see a Son who is completely consumed with love for His Father. Jesus calls Him *Abba*—the most tender Aramaic term that expresses an intimate relationship between a son and his father. And the good news is that Jesus invites us to share in that relationship. This is one of the greatest revelations we receive from Jesus. When His disciples asked Him how to pray, Jesus answered:

> *Pray then like this:*
> *"Our Father in heaven, hallowed be your name."*
> Matthew 6:9

This may not appear significant, unless we understand the backdrop of the story. When the disciples asked Jesus to teach them to pray, they were asking Him for a unique prayer that would serve as a token of their communion. By teaching them (and by extension us) to invoke God as "our Father," Jesus essentially authorized us to participate in His communion with God.[7]

While the notion of seeing a deity as "father" was not uncommon in antiquity, in Palestinian Judaism the word "Father" was seldom used to refer to God. When it was used, it was in a communal sense (as in "the Father of creation"; or "the Father of Israel") and it stressed their reverence and obligation to obey; but until Jesus there is no record of an individual addressing God as "my Father."[8]

By His referring to God as "my Father," Jesus breaks all the norms; and He goes even farther! Not only does He address God as "my Father," but He uses the term *Abba*. Some scholars hold that the use of the term *Abba* is itself indicative of the level of intimacy between Jesus and the Father. This was revolutionary! To a Jewish mind it would have been irreverent to use such an intimate term to address God. Jesus' usage was new, unique, and unheard of. Jesus spoke with God as a child speaks with his father, denoting intimacy and security. Jesus' special word for Father, *Abba*, conveys "a special relationship of treasuring and being treasured that simply cannot conceivably be broken."[9] Therefore, there is no doubt that when Jesus uses *Abba* to address God, He is revealing the very basis of their relationship.[10]

We can know God as our *Abba* who loves each of us uniquely and cares for us. The uniqueness of the disciples of Jesus is that, through Jesus, we get to participate in the communion of the Father, Son and Holy Spirit.[11] We can know God, not as the distant "Father of Creation," but as our *Abba* who loves each of us uniquely and cares for us. Thus, we can live in the security of His embrace.

Our challenge is that we tend to have wrong notions about the Father, so we build our doctrines on a faulty foundation. In fact, A.W. Tozer says that "there is scarcely an error in doctrine or a failure in applying Christian ethics that cannot be traced finally to imperfect and ignoble thoughts about God."[12] Another way of saying this is that what we believe about God affects what we believe about everything else. To correct this, I want to show you the Father through the eyes of Jesus. I want to introduce you to *Abba* through the eyes of the Son who came to make Him known.

What follows in the pages of this book is my contribution to help you grow in your relationship with *Abba*. In this book you won't find a list of things that you must do for the Father to be pleased with you. You won't find practical steps for developing disciplines that will make you a "good Christian." You won't find a list of doctrines that you must learn, as if there was some "cosmic quiz" at the end of our days that would determine whether we get to spend eternity with the Father. Instead, we will start by establishing the importance of a right perspective and explaining how Jesus gives us the clearest and most reliable picture of the Father. Then we will attempt to explore the heart of the Father through the eyes of Jesus by looking at God as a triune being, the Father and creation, the Father's will, the Father's mission, the Father and holiness, the Father and relationships, the Father and freedom, the Father's gifts, and the Father's call.

My hope is that these chapters will provide a firm foundation for an ongoing relationship between you and the Triune God, such that you will receive the love of Father, Son and Holy Spirit, experience increased freedom from fear, and be motivated and empowered for healthy relationships, obedience and service. This is the essence of discipleship and the key to abundant life.

One

A Matter of Perspective

He who has seen Me has seen the Father.

—Jesus

I am fascinated by optical illusions. I'm assuming you know what I'm talking about. These are graphic representations that trick our eyes into seeing something that's not really there—like moving lines, dancing dots, or changing colors—or forcing us to look twice to notice something that is there but that we miss unless we take a closer look. A well-known illusion is the simple silhouette that can represent either a rabbit or a duck, depending on how you interpret the picture. Another is a drawing of a woman's head that can be either a lovely young lady or an "old hag." Seeing both usually requires someone pointing out the details that give the visual clues for the interpretation. One of my favorites is a drawing of a beautiful bay in the background and a tree in the foreground. What is not readily apparent is that this is also a picture of a baby. Most people have a hard time finding the baby even though he takes up most of the page. They need a friend who will point out what is plainly visible but missed because their focus is elsewhere.

On a recent trip to Egypt we went to see the Great Pyramids of Giza and the Sphynx. Fascinating! During our camel ride in the desert, our camel handlers offered to take our picture in front of the pyramids. They get creative with these so they can earn tips, so they had us make awkward poses that didn't make any sense at the time. Once we saw the pictures I understood what they were doing. On one picture it seemed as though my fingertip was touching the tip of the Great Pyramid; on another one I look as though I'm lifting a huge rock; and my favorite is the one in which I am kissing the Sphynx. This, of course, is another type of optical illusion—pictures taken at a particular angle to present a distorted view of reality. These are good for a laugh, and make good conversation starters; but don't represent reality.

What we believe about God determines what we believe about everything else.

Could it be that we have other, more significant distorted views of reality that affect the whole of our lives? I am talking about our view of God. What we believe about God determines what we believe about everything else; so, before we go any further we must stop and ask whether we really know God, or if perhaps we have a distorted view of who God is. If God really is pure love, and yet I don't a have a craving to be with Him every second, could it be that I have a distorted view of Him?

We Need a Right View of God

Francis Schaeffer explains that a false view of God gives us a false view of reality with four significant consequences: it separates us from God, which is spiritual alienation; it separates us from ourselves, resulting in psychological imbalances; it separates us from one another, resulting in sociological conflict, and separates us from nature, resulting in ecological rape (or the misuse and abuse of natural resources). Think about this. Could it be that the most pressing problems we face in our world today stem from a distorted view of God?[13] Could it be that wholeness—spiritual, psychological, sociological and ecological—starts with a whole relationship with our heavenly Father, where we see Him as healthy, loving, forgiving, and accepting of who we are right now?[14] Could it be that the answer really lies with knowing God—Father, Son, and Holy Spirit—in an intimate relationship of love?

Perhaps at this point you are thinking about "those people out there" who don't know God. But I'm talking to you as well. You see, there is a big difference between knowing *about* God and *knowing* God.

In our modern Western setting, we tend to equate having information with knowing. In fact, the English language doesn't help us, because we use the same word "knowing" to denote both intellectual and experiential knowledge. Other languages are more specific; but we have this disadvantage. We have information at our fingertips, so we go about our lives collecting data, and somehow buy into the notion that because we have a lot of information about someone, we know her. This is one of the deceptions of social media.

Just because we read someone's encapsulated thoughts doesn't mean that we actually *know* the person. It only means that we have some glimpses into his way of thinking. Just because I can read the news articles about my favorite artist doesn't mean that I *know* her. It just means that I know *about* her. But I don't know these people like I

Could it be that we have perceived God to be different from how the Father reveals Himself?

know my husband. I spend time with him; I talk with him; we have cried and laughed together. We share our dreams, our hopes, and our fears. We have been on amazing adventures and worked through difficult seasons. We *know* each other in the truest sense of the word—not because we have information about each other, but because we have cultivated a relationship of knowing and being known.

Back to the issue of *knowing* God. Most Christians would claim that they *know* God, but is it possible that we have collected information and come to conclusions about God's way of being based on our own experience and observation? Could it be that we have perceived God to be different from how the Father reveals Himself? If we have a distorted view of God, it's difficult to develop this kind of intimate relationship of knowing and being known; so, we settle for getting our doctrine right—we'll even argue about it—and assume that by doing so, we have a relationship with God. But again, knowing *about* God and *knowing* God are two different things. Often, what gets in the way of us really *knowing* our Father is that we have faulty information about Him to begin with.[15] We have a problem.

I want to take some time to help us see clearly—to get rid of the optical illusions and find a way to restore our vision of God so we can develop a whole relationship with Him, in which we can be whole as well. (The companion book, *The Abba Factor* explains how God works in us to make us whole, delivering us from an orphan spirit and forming in us a spirit of sonship.) Let's start, if you will, by asking the question, "Where do we get our view of God?" Think for a moment about our sources.

Where Do We Get Our View of God?

Whenever I ask the question, "Where do we get our view of God?" most believers respond, "from the Bible." And, of course, God has revealed Himself through Scripture. The problem with this is that before we start reading the Bible, we already have some preconceived notions of what God is like. When we come to Christ, we think we come with a clean slate and we can get to know God objectively by reading the Bible; but what we often do is read the Bible through the lens of our preconceived view of God. I suggest to you that we have all been exposed to ideas about God from other sources; and when we read Scripture, we do so with a filter that simply reinforces our earlier notions about who God is. Think for a moment, what are some other sources that may have painted a picture of God—good or bad—that may be creating a distortion?

Art

Think about art, for example. Have you seen paintings of biblical stories? These are simply depictions of how the artist interprets the story; but when we see them, we subconsciously assume that they are accurate. Perhaps they are; perhaps they are not. We may not do this consciously, but art has a way of imprinting our minds with these ideas, which become filters for us and can hinder our relationship with God.

Entertainment

How about the entertainment world? Have you watched movies or TV programs about biblical stories or about God? Here, once again, we see interpretations—some accurate, some flawed. But they paint for us a picture of God's way of being; and whether we realize it or not, we may be projecting Hollywood's view of God on our own perception of who God is. The same can be said for music, or even politics.

Mythology

How about mythology? Could it be that we have developed notions about God from the gods of Roman or Greek mythology? Perhaps we perceive God as the Greek deity—Zeus—who dictates a natural, universal code of morality and does whatever He wants because He is dictating everything "for the best." Is this the way God really is?

Religion

For some of us, our view of God has been formed by religious experience. I grew up in a particular denomination that painted God as an old, angry king, sitting up in heaven on a distant throne, looking down to see how I behaved, and hurling down punishment whenever I did something wrong. It's difficult to develop a close relationship with a god like that!

Life Experiences

For many of us, our view of God has been formed by our experiences; in particular the trials of life. When we go through difficult things we look for explanations to help us deal with the pain, and for answers to the many questions we have.[16] However we resolve those issues forms in us a notion of who God is, and will have a direct impact on our relationship with Him. When God gives good things, we may see them as a sign of His interest and favor. We feel He is pleased with us, and thus we feel comfortably close to Him. But when we go through difficulties, we attribute that to God as well, interpreting it as a sign of his displeasure, rejection or vengeance. We feel cast off by God. When we evaluate our life with our limited understanding we perceive God to be fickle and unpredictable—in a good mood one day, and a bad mood the next. We don't know what He wants to do, so we either choose to stay away, or live in constant fear of His presence. We will cover that in greater detail later on.[17]

There are two other influences that I want to address in greater depth—one because we are often unaware of it; and the other because it's so significant that it deserves a longer explanation.

Roman, Greek, or Hebrew?

Whether we realize it or not, the Western Church has been afflicted by both Roman and Greek worldviews. Both have informed how we view and relate to God. Let's start with the Roman worldview, because it's the most prevalent in the Church today.[18]

Roman

The Roman society was pragmatic. Therefore, they emphasized authority and valued concrete thinking—right or wrong, good or bad, black or white. For the Romans, love is a choice. In the Roman worldview the Law is the system for control, and God is the Law-giver who inspires fear. The Bible is the book of law and punishment. Sin, of course, is breaking the Law; and salvation is primarily about Jesus taking the punishment that we deserve. Does that sound familiar?

Do you think Western culture is influenced by Roman thinking? What kind of buildings do you see in Washington D.C.? What do our cathedrals and monuments look like? Our national symbol, the bald eagle, is the seal of Rome.

What about our view of God? Can you think of any ways in which the Roman worldview has impacted how we think about God, sin, the Bible, or salvation?

When we hold a Roman view of God, we will be concerned with having the "right doctrine," teaching others how to think and act the "right way," and will be mostly concerned with punishment or the absence of it. As we shall see later, there is some truth to this; but this orientation produces fear and distance rather than a desire to know God intimately.[19]

Greek

Now let's look at the Greek worldview, which is also present in our context. The Greek society was contemplative. As such, they emphasized beauty and truth through abstract thinking. Remember that Philosophy developed in a Greek context. The Greek worldview holds that everything happens as it must happen, according to fate. Things are pre-determined and the key to happiness is reasonableness.[20] The goal is understanding natural law, and then judging and acting compatibly with it.

Through a Greek lens, God directs everything for the best, the Law is the principle of the universe and the Bible is the book that teaches us these principles, so if we put them in practice we can expect good outcomes. With this lens, we can be comfortable following Jesus as the good teacher He is; but this doesn't require relationship. For the Greek worldview love is a feeling, sin is choosing the physical over the spiritual, and salvation is the promise that we will someday leave this material world to spend eternity in heaven.

Love is neither a choice nor a feeling, but shared life.

Do you think Western culture is influenced by Greek philosophy? What kind of values do you see in our context that resonate with the Greek worldview?

What about our view of God? Can you think of any ways in which the Greek worldview has impacted how we think about God, sin, the Bible, or salvation?

When this is our worldview, we are more concerned with ethics and decency; what is pleasing and proper. There is still an emphasis on behavior, though the motivation comes from a different place. Again, there is some truth to the Greek lens; there is nothing wrong with good morals; but is that what being a disciple is all about? Contrast these two with the Hebraic orientation that developed as people lived in covenantal relationship with God.

Hebrew

The Hebrew society is relational, and as such, emphasizes covenant, belonging, and wisdom. Love is neither a choice nor a feeling, but shared life. It's about covenant and mutuality. When God revealed Himself to the people of Israel, He entered into covenant with them. In fact, God both initiated and fulfills the covenant, for the purpose of relationship. He is the covenanting God of promise and presence, and His Law is the expression of this covenantal relationship. I want you to note the emphasis on relationship in the Hebraic society, which is in stark contrast with the individualistic mindset of the West. For the Hebrew worldview, sin is the loss or injury of relationship; it's not knowing (experientially) one another. So, salvation is primarily about restoring relationship, bringing about wholeness in relationship with God and with one another.

I trust that by now you have identified many voices that lead us to have a distorted view of God. If you identify more with the Roman or Greek worldviews than the Hebrew, relational worldview, it's quite likely that your view of God is distorted. If you are feeling a bit uncomfortable, that is good! For it's only when we realize that we haven't been seeing clearly that we can do something about it. Before we move forward, however, we need to address one more source that forms our view of God—perhaps the most significant one, and usually the most damaging.

Earthly Fathers and Our Heavenly Father

A primary source of our view of God is our earthly father. It's no coincidence that God reveals Himself as "Father," even though the word can carry negative connotations. Many people have a hard time relating to God as a good Father because of their own experience with their earthly fathers. We know that there is no such thing as a perfect earthly father. Some are better than others; but none are perfect. Yet, even though we are aware of it, we tend to project onto God the characteristics of our earthly fathers. We must learn to make the distinction. A few examples may help us illustrate how this works (and by the way, if any of these rings true, please work through the forgiveness exercise at the end of the chapter before moving on to the next section).

Perhaps you had a father who was absent. Maybe he died when you were young, abandoned your mother, or had reasons beyond his control that kept him from being with you in your formative years. Maybe he was in the home, but worked long hours or traveled a lot. Or maybe he was present physically, but wasn't there when you needed him. Maybe he just didn't know how to have a deep conversation, how to answer your questions, or how to show you his love and affection. Maybe he only showed up—really showed up—when you were in need of correction. Any of these may lead you to project the same characteristics onto God. You may subconsciously think that God is the same—absent, distant, or disinterested. You may know in your mind that He is present; but have a hard time trusting that He will be there for you when you need Him. But *God is not like your earthly father.*

Perhaps your father wasn't a good provider. Maybe he didn't have a good work ethic and spent a lot of time between jobs. Maybe he was a hard worker but didn't know how to manage money. Maybe he had vices—drugs, drinking, gambling—that drained the family funds. Perhaps he just had an unfortunate economic reversal. Maybe he did the best that he could; but it just wasn't quite enough. Or maybe he had plenty of resources, but didn't know how to give without expecting anything in return. Maybe he wanted to teach you the **God is not like your earthly father.** value of hard work and set the expectation that you had to earn everything he gave you. If you grew in this atmosphere, you may project onto God the idea that He will not provide for your needs. You may feel that God

22

expects you to look out for yourself, make it on your own. But *God is not like your earthly father.*

Perhaps you grew up with a strict father who demanded perfection of you. No matter how hard you tried, you felt he was impossible to please. Maybe you struggled in school and felt like you were a disappointment. Maybe you were a good student, but your father only focused on where you could have done even better. Perhaps your father thought that the best he could do for you was teach you unquestioned discipline and absolute obedience, so no matter what you did, he kept raising the bar. Maybe your father just didn't know how to celebrate your successes. If this is the case, you may be projecting your father's attitudes, thinking that God expects the same from you. Maybe you are like so many who think no matter how hard you try, God will never quite be pleased with you. But *God is not like your earthly father.*

Perhaps you had the opposite experience and grew up with an over-indulging father. Maybe he wasn't around much; but whenever he came home, he showered you with gifts to compensate for his absence. Maybe he was afraid of hurting you, so he went to the other extreme and didn't correct you at all. Maybe he thought the best way to show you his love was by celebrating everything you did, no matter what. If this is your case, you may also have wrong expectations of God, misinterpreting God's correction or discipline as disappointment or lack of love. But *God is not like your earthly father.*

Maybe you are one of the fortunate few who grew up with an earthly father who knew how to be present, how to provide in healthy ways, how to discipline and correct in love, and how to encourage with boundaries. We would call that a "good father;" but Jesus says even these are evil by comparison to God, *the* Father (Luke 11:13). In Jesus' words and ministry we see Him on a mission to restore our view of the Father—His *Abba*—and He invites us to know Him, not through the lens of religion, or our experiences, or our cultural context, but through the eyes of the Son. How do we do that? We finish this chapter with answering that question.

If we want to know what God is like, we need only look at Jesus.

Where Do We Get the Right Image of the Father?

God provides a sure way for us to clear away any misunderstanding about who He is. The way is neither a method or system; nor a doctrine, nor Scripture itself. No. The way is a Person. Jesus himself is the way. Jesus is at the same time the representation of Father God (the God many of us see as distant and unreachable) and humanity (Jesus is human, subject to the same tangible world as we). In all four Gospels Jesus describes His relationship with His *Abba*, and portrays *Abba* God as a loving, caring and compassionate Father who dwells in Jesus' heart and who longs to dwell in ours.[21] Look at what the Bible says about Jesus:

> *No one has ever seen God,*
> *but God the One and Only,*
> *who is at the Father's side,*
> *has made him known.*
>
> John 1:18

Jesus is the One who came from the Father's side—from the place of most intimate relationship with the Father—and He has made the Father known to us. If we want to know what God is like, we look to Jesus.

> *He [Jesus] is the image of the Invisible God,*
> *the first born of all creation.*
>
> Colossians 1:15

We could say that Jesus is the high-def, 3-D image of the Father. He is the One who reveals to us, in a human manifestation, the character and being of God.

Look at this exchange between Jesus and His disciples:

> *Jesus said to him, "I am the way, and the truth, and the life.*
> *No one comes to the Father except through me. If you had known*
> *Me, you would have known My Father also; and from now on*
> *you know Him and have seen Him."*
> *Philip said to Him, "Lord, show us the Father,*

and it is sufficient for us."
Jesus said to him, "Have I been with you so long,
and yet you have not known Me, Philip?
He who has seen Me has seen the Father;
so how can you say, 'Show us the Father?'"
John 14:6-9

Jesus is emphatically saying that if we want to know what God is like, we need only look at Him [Jesus]. Here is one more statement that Jesus makes about himself that gives us a clear indicator that we can know the Father by looking at Jesus:

The Son [Jesus] can do nothing of his own accord,
but only what he sees the Father doing.
For whatever the Father does, that the Son does likewise.
John 5:19

Everything Jesus did and said is merely an extension of His Father. In other words, if we want to know what God the Father would say or do in any situation, we look to Jesus. If Jesus didn't do it, the Father won't do it, either. But sometimes we have ideas about God that are inconsistent with the Father that Jesus reveals.

Have you heard someone say, "This sickness is from God; He's testing me;" or "God gives and takes away;" or "God is teaching me a lesson?" What about, "Be careful what you ask for … if you ask God for patience, He's going to put you through something hard so that you can develop patience?" Now contrast that with what we see Jesus doing.

Do you ever see Jesus making someone sick to teach her a lesson? What did Jesus do with the sick who came to Him? Do you ever see Jesus saying, "You haven't been behaving up to my standards lately, so I won't feed you?" Or, "Sorry, but I can't heal you until you learn your lesson?"

Think about the logic of our thinking. We believe the Father makes someone sick to "test him;" but we see in the Gospels that Jesus was moved with compassion and healed the sick. Was Jesus acting in opposition to His Father's purposes? Or could it be that we misinterpreted the cause of the sickness?

We believe the Father always determines the appointed time for someone to die; but we see

If Jesus didn't do it, the Father won't do it, either.

25

in the Gospels that Jesus' ministry (and the ministry delegated to His disciples) includes raising the dead. Was Jesus defying His Father's will? Or could it be that we have made incorrect assumptions about the situation?

We believe the Father sends a storm to test the disciples; but we see that Jesus stilled the storm. Was Jesus being disobedient to the Father? Or could it be that we misunderstood the cause or purpose of the storm?

I know from personal experience that God certainly uses whatever we go through; but let's not confuse His using it, with it coming from Him or being His will. Jesus tells us that there is an enemy that comes to steal, kill and destroy (John 10:10). By contrast He says, "If you've seen me, you've seen the Father!" Whatever Jesus would do in any situation, that is the Father's will. Always!

Jesus is the perfect representation of God in human form. Said another way, **Jesus is perfect theology!**

Conclusion

In this chapter we have said that what we believe about God determines what we believe about everything else. Unfortunately, our view of God has been formed by art, entertainment, music, religion, politics, and our own experiences. It has also been impacted by the Roman worldview, which focuses on law, rules and regulations; and by the Greek worldview, which emphasizes abstract thinking and a separation of the spiritual and material worlds. Neither of these values relationships; which is the focus of the Hebraic worldview that reflects most closely God's way of being. Another source that impacts our view of our Heavenly Father is our relationship with our earthly father. All of these sources can result in a distorted view of the *Abba* of Jesus.

However, we also said that Jesus is the express image of the Father; so, if we want to know *Abba*, we look to Jesus. Jesus is perfect theology. As simple as this sounds, knowing that Jesus is the highest revelation of the Father is significant for us. This will be our foundation, and we will continue to build on this through the rest of this study.

REFLECTION

Talk with God and ask Him about ways in which you've had a wrong perspective about Him. Be silent for a moment and listen. You may get a word, a picture, a vision, or a general sense as a response. Agree with Him, confessing what He shows you and asking Him to open your eyes so you can know Him better.

Talk with God and ask Him what He wants to show you about Himself. How do you see Jesus responding to you? Be silent for a moment and listen. You may get a word, a picture, a vision, or a general sense as a response.

PRAYER

Father, we thank You for sending your Son, as Your perfect image, so that we can know You better. Thank You for sending Your Holy Spirit to live with us and to guide us into all truth. Open our spiritual eyes so we can see how we have held on to wrong ideas about You and show us Your heart more clearly. Give us eyes to discern where we have held on to distorted images of who You are, and give us a greater revelation of Your love. Give us a Spirit of wisdom and understanding to know You better. Enlighten the eyes of our understanding to know the hope to which You have called us, the riches of Your inheritance in us, and the incomparable greatness of Your power toward us, according to the working of Your mighty power. In Jesus' name we pray. Amen.

(see Ephesians 1:17-19)

Chiqui Wood

GROUP DISCUSSION

1. Our view of God is influenced by how He is portrayed in art and entertainment, music and politics, religion, and experiences. How have you seen God portrayed in movies? How is God portrayed in politics? How has religion impacted your view of God? How have your experiences shaped your view of God?

2. Think about Roman, Greek, and Hebrew worldviews. How does Roman thinking affect our view of God? How does Greek thinking affect our view of God? How does the Hebrew view give you a different sense of how God wants to relate to you?

3. God wants us to *know* Him. Discuss how you get to know somebody. If you were making a new friend, what would you do to get to know him better? What would you do to find out how he thinks or what he likes?

4. Jesus is perfect theology. How does this impact your view of God? Have you had experiences that may have distorted your view of God? How does seeing the Father through Jesus correct that view?

28

Forgiveness Exercise

I am mindful that the earthly father examples I mentioned earlier may be painful to you. If you had bad experiences with your father, whether I mentioned them or not, these may be impacting your relationship with God. But the perfect Father wants to heal you and make you whole. Forgiveness is the starting place for your own healing.

Take some time to talk to God about your earthly father. It's OK to be honest and mention the things that hurt you. You don't have to cover for him; if you were wounded, acknowledge the hurt. It may help to write it down. Now pray a prayer of forgiveness over him. You can say something like:

God, I choose to forgive my father, _____, for hurting me. I recognize the hurt and want to turn it over to You. I release my father from the prison of my heart and turn him over to You. I ask that You deal with him in Your perfect justice and that You heal my heart.

Now, if you are able, you can take this a step further and bless your father. There is something about blessing those who hurt us that works healing in our own hearts (Luke 6:27-28). Ask God to reveal Himself to him, to heal any wounds he may have, and to make him whole.

Some wounds run deep, and I don't presume that this simple prayer is all the healing you need. If you need further help, please see a Christian counselor who can help you work through these wounds. Ask your pastor for referrals in your area.

Two

Our Relational God

I pray for them, that they all may be one, as You, Father, are in Me, and I in You; that they also may be one in Us, that the world may believe that You sent Me.

—Jesus

Everything that God does is consistent with who He is, but we don't always connect the dots. If our view of God is skewed, so is our interpretation of what we experience, see, hear, or read. If we have a misconception about who God is, it will impact how we think about everything else, including creation and what it means to be created in God's image; God's will and the problem of evil; sin and holiness, salvation and redemption; and how to live as children of God. Therefore, we must start by laying the foundation of God's way of being. Then we can explore the rest.

Most books of systematic Theology describe God using terms such as omniscient, omnipresent, and omnipotent. These words are helpful in giving us an understanding that God is far greater than we can comprehend. He is not just a super-sized human. He is completely other. He is infinitely beyond our understanding. But they fall short of giving us a whole picture of who God is. We often try to understand our Heavenly Father based on His attributes, so we spend time defining and describing His actions, hoping that by doing so we can get to know Him. But God, our Father, is seen, felt, and understood in a close and personal relationship. When we focus on what God does we can miss the essence of who He is.

When I say, "who God is," I am talking about the Father, the Son, and the Holy Spirit. We cannot separate them. Father, Son, and Holy Spirit are three persons but one God. This is what we call the Trinity.

The Trinity

We use the term "Trinity" when referring to God; but don't always understand what it means or why it matters. The Trinity is a mystery. It's one of those big theological concepts beyond human comprehension; but it helps us understand that God, in His being, is first and foremost relational. The doctrine of the trinity is not incidental to our faith; it's essential. Let me explain what I mean and why it matters. We will start with some definitions and then make application.

Though the word "Trinity" doesn't appear in the Bible as such, there are many scriptures that reveal Father, Son and Holy Spirit acting together for the sake of their creation. Let's explore some:

> *In the beginning, God created the heavens and the earth.*
> *The earth was without form and void, and darkness*
> *was over the face of the deep. And the Spirit of God*
> *was hovering over the face of the waters.*
>
> *And God said, "Let there be light," and there was light.*
> Genesis 1:1-3

Notice the work of the Spirit in this creation account. Now combine that with John's description, where he refers to Jesus as "the Word:"[22]

> *In the beginning was the Word, and the Word was with God,*
> *and the Word was God. He was in the beginning with God.*
> *All things were made through him, and without him was not*
> *any thing made that was made.*
> John 1:1-3

By looking at both verses together, we see that the Father, Jesus, and Holy Spirit were all involved in the act of creation. Now look at the language used to tell the story of the creation of humanity:

> *Then God said, "Let us make man in our image, after our*
> *likeness." So God created man in his own image, in the image of*
> *God he created him; male and female he created them.*
> Genesis 1:26-27

The word translated as *God* is the Hebrew word *'elohiym*, which is a plural intensive with singular meaning.[23] The verse in the original language is conveying the idea that God is at the same time one and many. This gives us a glimpse of the relational way of being of God: the three-in-one; the one and the many. We see the mystery of the Trinity in Scripture from the start.

The Bible describes God as possessing both male and female qualities.

I want you to notice a few things. First, notice God saying, "our image" and "our likeness." We see Father, Son, and Holy Spirit working together. Second, notice that when God created "man" in God's image and likeness, He created both male and female. Though we use the male pronoun "He" to denote God, the Bible describes God as possessing *both* male and female qualities. We cannot assign a specific gender to God. In that sense, it's inappropriate to use "Him" or "Himself" as pronouns for God; but our language is limited, so we use available words to convey ideas that surpass our comprehension.[24] In creation we see that the union of both male and female together—unity in diversity—reflect the image and likeness of our Creator.[25] We will expand on this in the next chapter. Now look at the inauguration of Jesus' ministry:

> *And when Jesus was baptized, immediately he went up from*
> *the water, and behold, the heavens were opened to him, and he*
> *saw the Spirit of God descending like a dove and coming to rest on*
> *him; and behold, a voice from heaven said,*
> *"This is my beloved Son, with whom I am well pleased."*
> Matthew 3:16-17

Once again, it's easy to see the Father, Son [Jesus], and Holy Spirit working together. We can say that all that Jesus did in His earthly ministry was initiated by the Father and empowered by the Holy Spirit. Here is another instance where we see the Trinity at work:

> *But the Helper, the Holy Spirit, whom the Father will send*
> *in my name, he will teach you all things and bring to*
> *your remembrance all that I have said to you.*
> John 14:26

Here we hear Jesus speaking, and He tells us that the Father will send the Holy Spirit in Jesus' name to be our comforter, teacher and guide. Can we look at one more? Here is a description of Jesus' ministry:

How God anointed Jesus of Nazareth with the Holy Spirit and with power. He went about doing good and healing all who were oppressed by the devil, for God was with him.

Acts 10:38

In this verse once again we see the Father, Jesus, and the Holy Spirit working together on behalf of humanity. The Father doesn't do anything without the Son and the Spirit; the Son doesn't do anything without the Father and the Spirit; the Spirit doesn't do anything without the Father and the Son.[26]

As we see from those verses, God is Three-in-One; three Persons, one essence; all eternal, fully equal (as God), but fully distinct. So, we can say that the Trinity is the community created by our Heavenly Father, Son and Holy Spirit. One scholar describes the Trinity as "a mystery of personal connectedness."[27] Another says that the Trinity is "a unique community of Persons."[28] Yet another says that the Trinity is "a communion of three persons—*not individuals*—in mutually constitutive relations with one another."[29]

What's the point? Notice that God is not some isolated, lonely being. God is the communion of three persons. It's a mystery. We can't fully understand it with our finite minds (and that's OK); but we must know that Father, Son and Holy Spirit have existed eternally in a relationship of love and mutual self-giving.

God's very existence is relationship, and this is one of the things that makes our God unique. There is no other religion in the world that worships a God who is three-in-one. Only our God is a relational God, and this is why we can know, experience, and desire love. In fact, love can only exist because our God, who created everything, exists in relationship. God's way of being is the truest definition of love. In fact, John says:

Father, Son and Holy Spirit have existed eternally in a relationship of love and mutual self-giving.

God is love.

1 John 4:8

God doesn't just have an emotion called love. Love is not something that God does. It is who He is. Therefore, we can say that *love* is a way of being toward other persons. Love cannot exist in an isolated individual; it can only exist in a dynamic relationship of persons. Therefore *love*, in its purest form, is the relationship between three Persons: Father, Son and Holy Spirit. Because love is who God is, everything He does is motivated by love. This will be significant in the following chapters, as we explore what God does.

God's love is such that He can't keep it to Himself.

Can we go a little further? Let me share two more terms with you that will help us see God's relationality more clearly: *ekstasis* and *perichoresis*. We are about to dive in some deep, important waters. We'll be connecting the dots back to these descriptions of God in the rest of the book.

Ekstasis

We owe a great debt to the early Church Fathers who wrestled with understanding God's self-revelation and gave us language to begin to understand. Not that we will ever fully understand God; but thanks to their work, we can have glimpses of what God's love looks like.

The Cappadocian Fathers (Basil of Caesarea, Gregory of Nazianzus, and Gregory of Nyssa) used the term *ekstasis* to describe God's way of being. This Greek word is made up of *"ek,"* which means "out," and *"stasis,"* which means "way of being." By using this term to describe God, they were saying that God's way of being is one that is always "going out" in an overflow of personal, communal, and self-giving love.[30] In other words, God's love is such that He can't keep it to Himself; therefore, He is eternally sharing that love in a personal way.

In the New Testament we see that the Father loves the Son; the Son loves the Father; and the Spirit is a manifestation of the shared love between the Father and the Son. What does God do with that love? He doesn't keep it to Himself. Instead, God gives:

God so loved the world that He gave His only begotten Son.

John 3:16

As my mentor, Wess Pinkham, likes to say, "When God gives a gift, He wraps it in a Person. He doesn't just send a message. He sends a Person."

The picture we see from Jesus, and all throughout Scripture, is of this relational, loving, other-centered, "being in relationship" God who "can't keep Himself to Himself."

We are beginning to see what true love looks like. It's not the fickle, wavering, conditional, demanding, self-seeking emotion that we see portrayed in movies and romance novels. All our human notions of love pale when compared with God's way of being. God is the embodiment, the only true definition of love. To understand it a bit further, let's look at another term that describes God's way of being.

Perichoresis

Early Church theologians used the word *perichoresis* to describe the way in which Jesus could be both God and human at the same time—one interpenetrating the other without the integrity of either being damaged by the other.[31] This is another one of those mind-blowing thoughts. How can Jesus be fully God and fully man? We can't comprehend it, but this idea gives us some insights into God's relational way of being.

This word *perichoresis* can also be used to speak of the shared life of the Father, Son, and Holy Spirit. It speaks of mutual indwelling, or interpenetration. It describes how each Person of the Godhead empties Himself into the other in a continual act of self-giving. Some have said that God is not God apart from the way in which Father, Son and Spirit eternally give to and receive from each other what they essentially are.[32] This dynamic giving to and receiving from one another is the essence of love. Can you imagine what that looks like? What is the quality of life that the Father, Son, and Holy Spirit enjoy?

Perichoresis is often explained through the metaphor of a circle dance where Father, Son and Holy Spirit are sharing their love in mutual other-centeredness and self-giving, in perfect union and harmony.[33] I envision a dynamic "circle dance" where the Father is continually (and infinitely) pouring His love to Jesus and the Holy Spirit, while Jesus is pouring His love to the Father and the Holy Spirit; and the Holy Spirit is also loving on the Father and the Son.

In this dynamic each Person experiences abundance of love, joy, peace, affirmation, and acceptance. They lack nothing; they are completely whole. This is the definition of abundant life, eternal life. Life as God has it. And this is what God desires for you and me. Listen to Jesus as He prays for us:

> *"I do not ask for these only, but also for those who will believe*
> *in me through their word, that they may all be one, just as you,*
> *Father, are in me, and I in you, that they also may be in us,*
> *so that the world may believe that you have sent me. The glory*
> *that you have given me I have given to them, that they may be one*
> *even as we are one, I in them and you in me, that they may become*
> *perfectly one, so that the world may know that you sent me*
> *and loved them even as you loved me."*

John 17:20-23

Jesus is saying that He wants us to experience the oneness of relationship that the Triune God experiences in Himself. God wants us to experience the life of *perichoresis*. We participate in the *perichoresis* and experience the fullness of our humanity when we live in whole relationships with God and with one another. But I'm getting ahead of myself.

Conclusion

In this chapter we have said that God has existed eternally in a relationship of love and mutual self-giving. This is what we call the Trinity. The Trinity is the community created by our Heavenly Father, Jesus the Son, and the Holy Spirit. God is three persons, one essence; all eternal, fully equal, but fully distinct. God's way of being is *ekstasis*: always "going out" in an overflow of infinite, personal, communal, and self-giving love. The quality of life of the Trinity is the *perichoresis*, which can be described as a circle dance of shared love, mutual other-centeredness and self-giving, perfect harmony, joy, peace, affirmation, and acceptance.

If God is in fact first and foremost relational, as we have seen, then it follows that everything God does is consistent with His relational way of being.

See God as a zealous lover, yearning to share who He is with His creation.

37

The Father's creation, His will, His mission, His expectations and desires for you, His commandments, all flow out of His love. We will explore these in the coming chapters; starting with the Father and creation.

For now, I want you to recognize that God is not an angry, reluctant deity in need of appeasement—as we often think He is. Instead, I invite you to see God as a zealous lover, yearning to share who He is with His creation. Maybe He is not as interested in you learning to keep certain rules, or developing a good ethical and moral lifestyle as He is in you experiencing fullness of life.

I leave you with the lyrics to this song. Can you hear the Father's invitation? He wants you to join in the dance!

Lord of the Dance

I danced in the morning when the world was begun
I danced on the moon, and the stars and the sun
I came down from heaven and I danced on the earth
At Bethlehem I had my birth.

Chorus:
Dance, dance wherever you may be
I am the Lord of the dance (said He)
And I'll lead you all wherever you may be
And I'll lead you all in the dance (said He).

I danced for the Scribe and the Pharisee
They would not dance and they wouldn't follow me
I danced for the fishermen: James and John
They came with me and the dance went on.

I danced on the Sabbath and I cured the lame
The holy people said it was a shame
They whipped and they stripped and they hung me high
And they left me there on a cross to die.

I danced on the Friday when the sky turned black
It's hard to dance with the devil on your back
They buried my body and they thought I'd gone
But I am the life and I still go on.

They took me down but I leapt up high
I am the life that will never, never die
I'll live in you if you'll live in me
For I am the Lord of the dance (said He).

REFLECTION

Read Jesus' prayer and think about what Jesus is saying. What is the implication of this prayer? What does God want for you?

I do not ask for these only, but also for those who will believe in me through their word, that they may all be one, just as you, Father, are in me, and I in you, that they also may be in us, so that the world may believe that you have sent me. The glory that you have given me I have given to them, that they may be one even as we are one, I in them and you in me, that they may become perfectly one, so that the world may know that you sent me and loved them even as you loved me.

Father, I desire that they also, whom you have given me, may be with me where I am, to see my glory that you have given me because you loved me before the foundation of the world. O righteous Father, even though the world does not know you, I know you, and these know that you have sent me. I made known to them your name, and I will continue to make it known, that the love with which you have loved me may be in them, and I in them.

John 17:20-26

Talk with God and ask Him what He wants to show you about Himself. Be silent for a moment and listen. You may get a word, a picture, a vision, or a general sense as a response.

PRAYER

Father, thank You for revealing Yourself to us in such personal ways. Thank You for the many ways You show us Your love. Thank You for sending your Son, as the most perfect expression of Your love for us. Grant us, according to the riches of Your glory, to be strengthened with might through Your Spirit in our inner man, that Christ may dwell in our hearts through faith; and that we, being rooted and grounded in love, may be able to comprehend the width, and length, and depth and height of Your love. Help us to know the love of Christ which passes knowledge, that we will be filled with all Your fullness. In Jesus' name. Amen.

(see Ephesians 3:16-19)

GROUP DISCUSSION

In John 17:20-23 Jesus expresses His desire that we may be one as He and the Father are one.

1. What does it mean to be "one" as they are one? Could it be more than just agreeing with one another? Could it be that God wants us to experience the life of *"perichoresis"* (the relational wholeness of the Father, Son, and Holy Spirit)?

2. What would our family, church and/or community look like if we would live as a community of persons who participate in *perichoresis*?

Many scriptures allude to the conversation within the Trinity. If we look at Jesus' final discourse and prayer (John 13:31-17:26) we get a glimpse of the love shared between the Father, Son and Holy Spirit.

3. Have you ever thought of how Father, Son, and Holy Spirit relate to one another? What would their conversation sound like?

Three

The Father and Creation

Let us make man in our image, after our likeness.

—God

As I write this chapter, Kerry and I are spending a week in a beautiful cabin in the Ouachita National Forest (Oklahoma). During this lovely time of rest, relaxation and writing, we are enjoying the diversity of God's creation. In just a few short days we have seen deer, squirrels, rabbits, butterflies, a fox, a turtle, and several kinds of birds, including a woodpecker that, according to the Forest Ranger, is the only species of woodpeckers that drills his nest in live trees. (I had no idea there was more than one type of woodpecker).

In fact, God's creation is so diverse that there are over 50 species of rabbits; approximately 70 types of wolves; there are over 2,500 types of snakes documented throughout the world, over 25,000 known species of fish, roughly 28,000 different types of butterfly species, and well over 375,000 different types of plants. And some are yet to be discovered. And that's just our planet! We could talk about the size of the universe, the millions of galaxies, with stars, planets, comets, meteorites, and so much more!

When we think of God as Creator, we have a general idea of just how great He is; but with all our understanding, we are still limited and we tend to impose our limitations on Him. When we say that "nothing is impossible with God," do we really believe; do we really understand how great He is? Can we comprehend the reality that He created all of this by just speaking it into existence?

This leads me to ask a few questions. First, why did God create anything in the first place? Second, how does God feel about His creation? And third, what does it mean that we are created in God's image and likeness?

43

The Father Creates Out of Love

Why did God create? Sometimes we hear that God created us so we would worship Him. When we do this, we are projecting our human brokenness onto God. This idea portrays God as some egotistical being in need of adulation, which would mean that creation is a utilitarian means for God to satisfy a need. But as we said in our previous chapter, God is a loving relationality. In the relationship of Father, Son, and Holy Spirit is fullness of love, joy, peace, affirmation, and acceptance. God lacks nothing. In His relationality, God is completely whole. God doesn't create out of necessity or compulsion. God doesn't need us to need Him. He doesn't need our praise to satisfy some emotional hole. We can say that because God is whole in himself, God creates as a free act—not because He needs to, but because He wants to.[34] And why would God want to create?

Remember from our last chapter, that God's way of being is *ekstasis*—infinite, overflowing, outgoing, self-giving love. The love between the Father, Son, and Holy Spirit is such that He can't keep it to Himself. God creates as an overflow of the love shared among himself. Said another way, the act of creation naturally flows out of God's way of being. Because God is love, God is self-giving. Because God is self-giving, God willingly creates a universe that He can fill with Himself and upon which He can pour His love.[35]

If God creates everything out of love and for love, it follows that God delights in His creation. Let's look at the Genesis account to see if this is the case.

The Father Delights in His Creation

In Genesis 1:1-31 we find the creation narrative. Let's look briefly at the different stages, and I want you to notice what the Bible specifically says about all God creates. This gives us an idea of how the Father feels about what He has created.

Because God is self-giving, God willingly creates a universe that He can fill with Himself and upon which He can pour His love.

In the beginning, God created the heavens and the earth.

Genesis 1:1

This was the starting point. He spoke everything into existence. At this point the earth was without form and void, and there was darkness.

> *And God said, "Let there be light," and there was light.*
> *And God saw that the light was good.*
>
> Genesis 1:3-4

This is the first instance in which we see God reflecting on His creation. What did God think about the light He created? He said that it was *good*.

On the second day God separated the waters, and in doing so He created an expanse called Heaven, earth and seas.

> *God called the dry land Earth, and the waters that were gathered together he called Seas. And God saw that it was good.*
>
> Genesis 1:10

How did God feel about the earth and the seas? Again, God saw that it was *good*. Then, on the third day …

> *The earth brought forth vegetation, plants yielding seed according to their own kinds, and trees bearing fruit in which is their seed, each according to its kind. And God saw that it was good.*
>
> Genesis 1:12

How did God feel about the vegetation? Once again, God saw that it was *good*. Are you seeing a trend here? Let's go further. On the fourth day God created the sun, moon and stars.

> *And God set them in the expanse of the heavens to give light on the earth, to rule over the day and over the night, and to separate the light from the darkness. And God saw that it was good.*
>
> Genesis 1:17-18

So far, we have seen that God deemed that light, the earth and the seas, vegetation, and the celestial bodies are all *good*. On the fifth day, God created animals, starting with sea creatures and birds.

So God created the great sea creatures and every living creature
that moves, with which the waters swarm, according to their
kinds, and every winged bird according to its kind.
And God saw that it was good.

Genesis 1:21

He said that these were *good*; but He didn't stop there. Next, He created more animals:

And God made the beasts of the earth according to their kinds
and the livestock according to their kinds, and everything
that creeps on the ground according to its kind.
And God saw that it was good.

Genesis 1:25

We have covered the first five days of creation and, so far, everything that God creates He declares *good*. Can you imagine the conversation between the Father, Son, and Holy Spirit as they reflect on their creation? I can hear the Holy Spirit say to the Father, "The way you just spoke things into being is amazing!" Jesus says to the Holy Spirit, "The way you hovered over the waters was awesome!" And the Father says to Jesus, "I couldn't have done it without you!" OK. Maybe it didn't sound exactly like that; but you get the point. God delights in His creation. At every stage of creation God is declaring that it is *good*.

Then we come to the sixth day. This is a significant day, so we will look at this one in greater detail.

Then God said, "Let us make man in our image,
after our likeness. And let them have dominion over the fish
of the sea and over the birds of the heavens and over the livestock
and over all the earth and over every creeping thing that creeps on
the earth." So God created man in his own image, in the image of
God he created him; male and female he created them.
And God blessed them. And God said to them, "
Be fruitful and multiply and fill the earth and subdue it,
and have dominion over the fish of the sea and over the birds of the
heavens and over every living thing that moves on the earth."

Genesis 1:26-28

Notice that God created humanity—man *and* woman—with a specific purpose. We are neither an accidental creation nor an afterthought. We will explore this shortly. For now, let's finish this portion of Scripture. After creating humanity ...

> *And God saw everything that he had made,*
> *and behold, it was very good. And there was evening*
> *and there was morning, the sixth day.*
>
> Genesis 1:31

Did you notice the change here? Throughout the first five days of creation, God said it was *good*. But after He creates humanity, as His partners to rule creation, God says it is *very good*. The Hebrew expression is *towb meod*, which means exceedingly, greatly, up to abundance, good, pleasant, excellent, and valuable.[36]

What is it about humanity that elevates creation from *good* to *exceedingly, greatly, abundantly good*? The fact that we are made in God's image and likeness. God created us differently from the rest of creation, and has given us unique characteristics.[37] Unlike anything else that has been created, only humans have in their being the imprint of God's own way of being.

Humans are the only created beings that have the capacity to receive God's love and to love Him in return. We have been created with free will, so we can share in His love but aren't obligated to do so. We are the only created beings who have the capacity to create, the capacity of abstract thought and invention, the capacity for faith, and the ability to appreciate beauty and create music and art. God created us in His image and likeness with the express desire that we would share with Him in caring for His creation. God wants to partner with us!

This is mind-blowing to me! Our Father, who created the universe by speaking it into existence, has chosen to partner with us—finite, fallible, limited beings. What could we possibly contribute to God's plan? Not much. But He delights in sharing all of creation with us, because that is who He is. God is love, so He creates *out* of love, *through* love, and *for* love.

Think of when you create something. How easy is it to give it to someone else to take care of? Think of

God created us with the express desire that we would share with Him in caring for His creation.

47

mothers with their babies and how long it takes before the baby can spend the night away from home. Think of children with their "masterpieces" and how protective they are of them. Think of how protective we tend to be with the things we "create"—our own "masterpieces." We want to protect them from those who could destroy them. We are controlling; but God isn't. His love is such that He delights in giving and sharing even if it's risky, as we shall see in the next chapter.

By looking at the Genesis story of creation we have established that God delights in His creation. It's in keeping with His way of being to create out of love, and to delight in what He has created. This includes you!

The Father Delights in You

The Father loves you because He created you. Think about the rest of creation. The stars and moons, plants and animals don't have to do anything to earn God's love. They just have to be. This became real to me as we were hiking in the Grand Canyon a few months ago.

We were admiring the majestic landscape—rock formations so massive that their size can't be grasped. And then I saw it. A little white flower, growing out of a rock, hidden under a bush. I wondered how many visitors walked by it without even noticing it. It wasn't clamoring for attention. It couldn't begin to compare with the greatness of its surroundings. But I was keenly aware that God noticed it, and I felt His delight for that little flower—because He created it, and because it was simply living out its design. Could it be that the Father feels the same way about you?

In Jesus' earthly life we see how the Father feels about His children. In Matthew 3 we see the story of the baptism of Jesus.

> *And when Jesus was baptized, immediately he went up from*
> *the water, and behold, the heavens were opened to him, and he saw*
> *the Spirit of God descending like a dove and coming to rest on him;*
> *and behold, a voice from heaven said, "This is my beloved Son,*
> *with whom I am well pleased."*
> Matthew 3:16-17

This was none other than the voice of the Father, beholding His Son and expressing His delight. Notice that at this point Jesus hadn't preached a single sermon; He hadn't healed anyone, cast out any demons, or done any miracles. And yet the Father declares that He is well pleased with Jesus, based not on performance but relationship. This is the heart of *Abba* toward His children— and that includes you!

The Father's love for you is not based on your performance.

The Father's love for you is not based on your performance. He is not comparing you with other people or measuring you on the basis of your achievements. He is not even weighing your response to His love. He loves you. Period. In fact, to say that *Abba* loves you is an understatement; He delights in you. *Abba* loves everything about you. He took great care in forming you and had great things in mind for you from the very beginning of your existence. Can you hear the Father say, "this is my beloved son (or daughter) with whom I am well pleased?" He is pleased because He made you; and He is pleased with the uniqueness of who you are.

There are many things about you that make you unique. Many of these are things that you didn't choose and that you can't change—like your family of origin, gender, time and place in history, language and culture, or personality traits. However, these can be seen as God's "seal of ownership" over you. Sometimes we resent the way God made us and go through life comparing ourselves with other people and wishing we were different. But I want you to see that God created you uniquely, with a purpose in mind. Look at how David expresses it:

> *For you formed my inward parts;*
> *you knitted me together in my mother's womb.*
> *I praise you, for I am fearfully and wonderfully made.*
> *Wonderful are your works;*
> *my soul knows it very well.*
> *My frame was not hidden from you,*
> *when I was being made in secret,*
> *intricately woven in the depths of the earth.*
> *Your eyes saw my unformed substance;*
> *in your book were written, every one of them,*
> *the days that were formed for me,*
> *when as yet there was none of them.*
> Psalm 139:13-16

49

> **You didn't do anything to deserve God's love; and therefore, there is nothing you can do to keep Him from loving you.**

When the Father created you, he looked at you and said, *"very good."* In fact, even now He looks at you and says, *"very good."*

Now, you may look at your life and say that it hasn't been good at all. It's possible that there are specific characteristics of your body or personality that you dislike. It's possible that you have had traumatic experiences, and you would be right in saying that your life hasn't been good. This doesn't mean that God likes everything that is going on in your life (we will address this later); but that He sees His fingerprints on your life and He sees the potential that He placed in you. He sees the dreams that have not been fulfilled yet; He sees what He has destined you to be—what He desires for you. And He says, it is *very good*. And *Abba* calls you to Himself so He can fulfill in you the very plans He had in mind when He created you.

If there's one thing I want you to remember from this is that you didn't do anything to deserve God's love; and therefore, there is nothing you can do to keep Him from loving you. He just wants you to be you, and to know how much He loves the unique person you are.

Before we leave this chapter, there is one more aspect of the Father and creation that I need to bring up because it's foundational to the rest of our study. It has to do with being created in God's image.

We Are Created in God's Image

In the last chapter we saw that God is Three-in-One: three Persons, one essence; all eternal, fully equal (as God), but fully distinct. We also said that God has His being in relationship. God is who He is by virtue of relationship—the relationship of love between the Father, Son, and Holy Spirit. In this chapter we looked at the Genesis account and see that when God created humanity, He said, "Let us make man in our image, after our likeness."

Imago Dei is the Latin phrase for "Image of God." It is used to describe the way in which humans are made in God's image and reflect His being. What does that look like? Earlier we described how humans are different from the rest of creation in our free will, our capacity for love, creativity, imagination, abstract thought, and faith. But most significantly, we are made—in God's image—as relational beings. If God's way of being is relationship, it follows that we are made for relationship as well, making it impossible to conceive of humans as isolated, individual entities.

Why do we need to bring this up? I'm sure it's not surprising to you to hear that we live in an individualistic culture.[38] Some common slogans in our culture teach us to "Always look out for number one;" "Never forget that only dead fish swim with the stream;" or "Take the time to simplify *you* to make *your* life better." We are bombarded with notions of making it on our own, being different from the crowd, and focusing on ourselves. In fact, the largest section of books in a bookstore may be the *self-help* section.

In a 1984 monograph titled, *The Values Americans Live By*, L. Robert Kohls describes the top 13 American values. Not surprisingly, the first is individualism. Because we value individualism, we also value privacy. Would it surprise you to know that the word "privacy" doesn't even exist in many languages? If it does, it's likely to have a strongly negative connotation, suggesting loneliness or isolation from the group. But for most of us, individualism is so ingrained, that we tend to think we are only slightly influenced by family, church, schools, or any other group. If and when we join a group, we tend to believe that we're just a little different, just a little unique, just a little special, from other members of the same group. We tend to leave groups as easily as we enter them. We only see the value of the group "if there is something in it for me."[39]

Where does this come from? Much of the prevalent Western thought derives from a Stoic concept of God as the giver of natural law which elevates the place of reason in the concept of personhood, leading to a false concept of personhood as individuality. Boethius (c. A.D. 480-525) stated, *"persona est individua substantia rationabilis naturae"* (a person is an individual substance of a rational nature). Notice that there is no mention of relationality in this definition. Instead, Western thought elevates reason as the determinant of what it means to be a person. In fact, according to the Stoics, a virtuous person is self-sufficient and happy. Does that sound familiar? Stoicism is a form of Greek philosophy. It's part of the Greek worldview.[40] Remember what we learned about the Greek influence on our culture in the first chapter? Therefore, the value we place on individualism derives from a concept of God that is contrary

We are only fully persons when we are in whole relationships, both with God and with our fellow humans. to the loving relationality of the Father, Son, and Holy Spirit. But it didn't stop there.

Then came the Enlightenment, which exalted the value of reason, so we end up with a tradition that equates the concept of "person" with "individual," focusing primarily on reason. We think if we just had more information, better information, we would make better decisions and our world would be a better place. But we're inundated with information, and our relationships are the worse for it. Again, this is all contrary to God's way of being.

Because of these Western notions, the *Imago Dei* has been understood individualistically. We may acknowledge the need for a vertical relationship (humans and God), but largely discount the need for horizontal relationships (with one another).[41] However, since God is a relational being, then it follows that we cannot conceive of a person as an individual. We are only fully persons when we are in whole relationships, both with God and with our fellow humans.

Humanity enjoys full personhood only in the context of relationships. Said another way, personhood is understood as the full reflection of God's way of being as a being-in-relation—whole in the context of a loving relationality. This means that it's impossible for a person to live fully as an isolated individual. There can be no such thing as an individual person. You cannot be wholly yourself without other people. Your personhood is established in relationship with others, not in the "I" but in the "You and I."

Let's go back to the Genesis narrative. In the account of creation, we see that persons are intrinsically related, not just to God but also to one another. Notice that when God created humanity, in His image, He created both male and female. Man—alone—is not made in the image of God. Neither is woman. When God created Adam, He said it was *not good* for man to be alone. In fact, this is the only part of creation where God said, "It is not good." Adam was not complete without a counterpart with whom to share life. In this sense, Adam became truly human when he greeted and accepted Eve—an equal but distinct human. Even now, the most perfect reflection of God's way of being is when man and woman willingly come together in love to serve one another and share life. This is expressed fully in marriage (at least, it's supposed to be), but is not exclusive to marriage. The same can be seen in relationships with

our family members, or among friends. The point is
that we reflect the *Imago Dei* in relationships with
one another, and particularly in relationships of
complementary differentiation. Said another way, to
be persons, in the fullest sense of the word, we need
others who are different from us.[42]

Human personhood is perfected in knowing and being known.

When we live in wholeness of relationships, we experience full
personhood—truly being who God has created us to be. Our significance
comes when we see that others have need of who we are and what we have
to give. And we need others who are gifted in areas where we lack. When
we willingly give and receive from one another, we are complete.[43] Let me
give you a couple of examples:

My friend Erin is a fantastic hostess. She loves decorating, preparing
food, and creating a welcoming atmosphere. This is how God designed
her. And I have been a grateful beneficiary of her gift (especially since it's
a gift I lack). But *she can't be who she is in isolation.* The fullness of her
being is expressed when she has others with whom she can share her gifts.

My friend Mauricio is a painter. He creates some amazing works of
art and comes alive when he gets to share his painting with others, talk
about them, and describe why he used certain colors or shapes. *He can't
be who he was designed to be in isolation.* The fullness of his being is
expressed when he has others with whom he can share his gifts.

My friend Johana is a songwriter. She loves to play piano or guitar;
but mainly she loves to write songs. We love it when she comes to our
home and asks to borrow Kerry's guitar. We know we're in for a treat.
When she sings one of her new songs, she beams. She needs others who
receive the gift she has to offer. And we are happy beneficiaries of her
gift. But *she can't be who she is in isolation.* The fullness of her being is
expressed when she has others with whom she can share her gifts.

We can say that in God's plan for humanity, we not only have
relationship with God, but with one another. Human personhood is
perfected in knowing and being known. Paul says:

> *Then I shall know fully, even as I have been fully known.*
> 1 Corinthians 13:12

Because we are created in God's image, we are made to live in
relationship, to find our significance in relationships. We enjoy fullness

of life in whole relationships with others, different from us, who complement us. We shall see later that all of God's commandments have to do with whole relationships.

Conclusion

In this chapter we said that God doesn't create out of necessity or compulsion. He creates, not because He needs to, but because He wants to. Since God's way of being is *ekstasis*—outgoing, self-giving love—God can't keep it to himself, so the act of creation naturally flows out of God's overflowing love way of being. By looking at the Genesis account we established that God delights in His creation, and especially in the creation of humanity—male and female—made in His image and likeness, and created for the purpose of relationship and partnership.

We also said that God delights in who you are, simply because you are His. You didn't do anything to deserve God's love; and therefore, there is nothing you can do to keep Father, Son, and Holy Spirit from loving you. Finally, we said that humans, created in the *Imago Dei*, are relational by nature. Contrary to what our individualistic culture may promote, humanity enjoys full personhood only in the context of relationships. Our significance comes when we see that others have need of who we are and what we have to give.

One final thought. Because we are made in the image of God, as we know one another better, we know God better. Have you had the experience of knowing someone to a certain degree—and then you meet their children, or their parents, or their siblings... and then you say, "Oh, now I know why you do this or that?" We get to know one another better as we get to know the people whom they are in relationship with. It's the same with God. As we know God, we come to know ourselves and one another better; and as we know one another, we know God better.

REFLECTION

Have you considered that when God created you, He declared you to be *very good*? Is this your experience? Do you know how much God loves you? Do you feel God's delight in who you are?

Ask the Father to show you specific things about you that He delights in. You can ask Him questions like the following:

- Father, when You were forming me in my mother's womb; what dreams did You have for me?
- Father, what is something about me that puts a smile on Your face?
- Father, when You look at my life, what are some things that You are proud of?
- Father, what is it about me that makes me unique and special?
- Father, what gifts did You put in me so I can share with those around me?

You may also want to talk to Him about ways to accept yourself more fully:

- Father, are there some characteristics of myself that I have rejected?
- Father, is there something You want to tell me about myself that I haven't thanked You for?

I encourage you to take time to journal what you hear the Father speaking to you. In the years to come you'll be able to read them and receive His love and affirmation all over again.

PRAYER

Father, I thank You for creating me with such great care. I acknowledge and celebrate how You knit me together in my mother's womb. I praise you because I am fearfully and wonderfully made. Because I am Your work, I know that I am wonderful. Show me if there are any aspects of who I am that I have resented. Forgive me from rejecting the way You made me and help me to see myself through Your eyes; that I would know how to appreciate everything about the way You made me. Teach me how to live in the fullness of the plans You had for me as you were forming me. I set myself in agreement with You about who I am, and I receive Your love and acceptance. In Jesus' name. Amen.

(see Psalm 139:13-14)

GROUP DISCUSSION

1. Think about the vast number of creatures on our planet. 50 species of rabbits; 70 types of wolves; 2,500 types of snakes; 25,000 types of fish or 28,000 types of butterflies. What does that tell us about God?

2. What does it say about us when God created us with the express purpose that we would join Him in taking care of everything He created? How do you think we have done in this partnership? What are some specific ways in which we could take better care of God's creation?

3. How does individualism hinder us from experiencing the fullness of life that the Father intends for us? What can you do, specifically, to cultivate more meaningful relationships?

Four

The Father's Will

I do nothing by myself; I only do what I see my Father doing,
because whatever my Father does, I also do.

—Jesus

In the last chapter we saw that at every stage of creation, God said that it is "good," "good," and finally, with the creation of humanity—God's partner—it is "very good." But if we take a close look we could say that many of the things that happen in our planet are "not good."

In 1980, a major volcanic eruption occurred at Mount St. Helens, in the state of Washington. In 1985 thousands died from volcanic-related mudslides in Colombia. In 2004 over 200,000 people died in the Indian Ocean earthquake and tsunami. Hurricane Katrina flooded the city of New Orleans in 2005. Haiti was destroyed by an earthquake in 2010. Afghanistan suffered devastating avalanches in 2015. These are just a few of thousands of natural disasters that have plagued our planet throughout history. When we hear of such disasters, how can we say that God's creation is "very good?"

The same can be said for our personal lives. Examples abound of murder, rape, abuse, accidents, and death. We see that in human history wars, poverty, extortion, slavery, and exploitation abound. How can we say that this is "very good?" When God created you, He said, "very good." But perhaps it seems your life has been anything but that. How do we make sense of this conflict?

I know from personal experience the many questions that come to mind when we face unexplainable loss. When I was 17, my 15-year-old cousin died suddenly. Eight months later, his father died. My sister's first baby was born with a terrible heart defect. He died 17 days later. In 2002, in our tenth month of marriage, my husband Hannibal was diagnosed with inoperable, incurable, terminal prostate cancer. He died 5 years later.

By looking at Jesus, we can surmise what is (and what isn't) the Father's will.

I could go on. But the point is that I am no stranger to wrestling with the questions of, "What happened? Is this what God wanted? If so, why? And if it wasn't, why did it happen? Where was God? Why didn't He do something about it?"

Before we get into it, I must admit that I write this chapter with some trepidation. Many scholars, with much better insight than me, have discussed the issue of God's will at length.[44] Trying to address it in one chapter is beyond the scope of this book. However, I am mindful that it needs to be addressed, because many of our skewed views of the Father result from trying to give explanation for the bad things that happen all around. So, I write about the Father's will, but not as a comprehensive treatise. I know from personal experience that there is an element of mystery in God's working on earth, through human partnership, to bring about His purposes.

Our finite human understanding demands answers for complex problems. I can see the Father smiling at us, lovingly saying, "some things are just beyond your understanding." It might be like having an astrophysicist explaining rocket science to a 2-year old. And it's probably much worse than that! How can we, finite beings, comprehend how God takes the billions of decisions free-willed humans make every second, and still somehow use the stuff of those decisions to work His plan? I don't know. But I do know that Jesus says:

Whoever has seen me has seen the Father.

John 14:9

So, there is at least some sense in which, by looking at Jesus, we can surmise what is (and what isn't) the Father's will. Jesus himself tells us that the Father is good:

If you then, who are evil, know how to give good gifts to your children, how much more will your Father who is in heaven give good things to those who ask him!

Matthew 7:11

Based on Jesus' own declaration, I write with the conviction articulated by Brennan Manning:

Abba is not our enemy. If we think that, we are wrong. Abba does not prefer and promote suffering and pain. If we think that, we are wrong. Abba is not intent on trying and tempting and testing us. If we think that, we are wrong. Jesus brings good news about the Father, not bad news.[45]

First, let's explore the Father's will by looking at Jesus, and what He reveals. Then we will discuss how we can partner with God in the accomplishment of His will.

What Happened to God's Good Creation?

As we have seen, we live in a world where bad things happen. When God created everything, He created it "very good." But now something has happened, and we want to know the cause. Whenever we see destruction—both at the macro and micro levels—well-meaning people try to comfort us by saying, "God is in control." There is truth in that; but it's usually stated with shrugged shoulders, implying both that God caused it, and that if He caused it, it's for a very good reason. This is supposed to be a comforting thought, but it bothers me. It simply doesn't make sense that God himself is destroying His own creation.

Imagine a human artist taking months to finish her masterpiece. On the day of its unveiling, it's widely praised. She is proud. She says it's "very good." She is satisfied with her work. Then she takes a knife and starts cutting through it, lights it on fire, and pours water on it. She then sits back with a grin on her face. We would say she is out of her mind! And yet we accept the notion that God acts the same way without question. Our theology is skewed.

From where do we get such notions? Perhaps we get them from Job, who said:

> *"The Lord gave, and the Lord has taken away;*
> *blessed be the name of the Lord."*
>
> Job 1:21

And later he asks:

"Shall we receive good from God, and shall we not receive evil?"
Job 2:10

It is true that Job said these things. He was wrestling, as we do, with trying to understand what was happening to him. In his very limited understanding of God he attributed everything—good or bad—to God.[46] But later in the story we hear God himself speaking. God asks Job:

"Who is this that darkens counsel by words without knowledge?"
Job 38:2

And again, calls him to account asking:

"Will you even put me in the wrong?
Will you condemn me that you may be in the right?"
Job 40:8

Notice that God is correcting Job's theology. Job accepts that correction and finally admits:

"I have uttered what I did not understand, things
too wonderful for me, which I did not know."
Job 42:3

If we are to derive our theology from Job, let's do so from the end of the book, acknowledging there are things beyond our understanding. But, as we said earlier, it's much better for us to derive our theology from Jesus. Remember: Jesus is perfect theology!

Notice a few things we learn from Jesus. First, Jesus teaches us to pray:

"Our Father in heaven hallowed be your name.
Your kingdom come, your will be done, on earth as it is in heaven."
Matthew 6:9-10

This begs the question, "If everything that happens is the Father's will, then why do we need to pray for His will to be done?" Jesus isn't teaching us to pray a senseless prayer. Instead, He is teaching us to cooperate with the Father. In Heaven, God's will is done perfectly. Therefore, in

Heaven there is neither sickness nor pain, neither crying nor suffering. Where God's will is done, the outcome is always good; but on earth, it's a different story. Not everything that happens is God's will. Therefore, we are instructed to pray that it will be so. We will look at this later in this chapter. For now, let's see what else we can learn from Jesus' ministry.

Second, when James and John, the "sons of thunder," asked Jesus if they could bring fire from heaven to consume the Samaritans who rejected Him, how did Jesus respond?

> [Jesus] *turned and rebuked them. And he said, "You do not know what manner of spirit you are of; for the Son of Man came not to destroy people's lives but to save them."*
> Luke 9:55-56

The disciples thought they could use Jesus' power to destroy; but Jesus says His power is only used to restore. Jesus denies His power for destruction, correction, discipline, or punishment. What we see in His ministry is that He only used it for restoration. Since Jesus says when we see Him we've seen the Father, it would be inconsistent to think that now God uses His power differently.

Third, when it comes to destruction, Jesus gives us understanding of what is happening behind the scenes, in the spirit realm:

> *The thief comes only to steal and kill and destroy. I came that they may have life and have it abundantly.*
> John 10:10

Notice the contrast. Jesus says whenever we see stealing, killing and destruction, this is not His doing. There is an enemy; but it's not Jesus. In fact, Luke tells us that Jesus' mission was the opposite:

> *How God anointed Jesus of Nazareth with the Holy Spirit and with power. He went about doing good and healing all who were oppressed by the devil, for God was with him.*
> Acts 10:38

Jesus went around doing good because the Father was with Him. His ministry stands in opposition to the work of the devil. Peter reinforces

When we have suffered, He restores us, makes us strong, firm, and steadfast. this idea when he writes to comfort the Church who is enduring severe persecution. Notice that Peter spells out clearly what is taking place and who does what:

Be sober-minded; be watchful. Your adversary the devil prowls around like a roaring lion, seeking someone to devour. Resist him, firm in your faith, knowing that the same kinds of suffering are being experienced by your brotherhood throughout the world. And after you have suffered a little while, the God of all grace, who has called you to his eternal glory in Christ, will himself restore, confirm, strengthen, and establish you.

1 Peter 5:8-10

Who is the enemy? The devil. What does the devil do? He creates suffering. What does God do? When we have suffered, He restores us, makes us strong, firm, and steadfast. Where the devil brings sickness, Jesus brings healing. Where the devil brings oppression, Jesus brings deliverance. Where the devil brings destruction, Jesus brings restoration.

It is true that we often see a lot of good come out of unspeakable tragedy. But that doesn't mean God orchestrated the tragedy, or that He needed it in order to bring about something good. Just because we see a good outcome doesn't mean the suffering was God's will. I have yet to find any place in Scripture that shows Jesus making anyone sick or orchestrating any kind of destruction.

Jesus says if we've seen Him, we've seen the Father. What we see, over and over, is that the Father, the Son, and the Holy Spirit are never causing destruction. Quite the contrary, they are on a mission of restoration. We will expand on this in the next chapter.

For now, let's look at some possible explanations of why bad things happen, despite God's will to the contrary.

Why Do Bad Things Happen?

We can say bad things happen because of (a) Satan's direct attack; (b) the exercise of our free will; or (c) because we live in a broken world, and suffer the effects of the cumulative effect of humanity's sin. Let's look briefly at each of these.

Satan's Direct Attack

As we have seen, Jesus says (and Peter confirms) that much of the suffering we endure comes from Satan. He is the enemy that comes to steal, kill and destroy; and he has legal authority to work on the earth.[47] To understand this, we need to go back to God's original design, where, in His sovereignty, God chose to give humans dominion over the earth. Using our God-given authority, humanity handed over that dominion to Satan. We see this clearly in several places. First, we see Jesus' affirmation of Satan's domain when He was being tempted:

> *Again, the devil took him to a very high mountain and showed him*
> *all the kingdoms of the world and their glory. And he said to him,*
> *"All these I will give you, if you will fall down and worship me."*
> *Then Jesus said to him, "Be gone, Satan! For it is written,*
> *"'You shall worship the Lord your God*
> *and him only shall you serve.'"*
>
> Matthew 4:8-10

Notice Jesus didn't deny Satan's claim that the kingdoms of the world belong to him, and that he has authority to give them back to Jesus (the rightful heir). While Jesus acknowledged the world is under the control of a usurper, He said He would not bow down to worship Satan. Jesus knew the price He had to pay to reclaim for God what humanity relinquished.

A few other places show where Jesus recognizes Satan's authority to rule in the world:

> *Now is the judgment of this world;*
> *now will the ruler of this world be cast out.*
>
> John 12:31

> *I will no longer talk much with you, for the ruler of this world*
> *is coming. He has no claim on me.*
>
> John 14:30

Because we have free will, the Father won't impose His will on us.

And when [the Holy Spirit] comes, He will convict the world … concerning judgment, because the ruler of this world is judged.

John 16:8, 11

Whom is Jesus talking about in these three instances? Satan. And Jesus calls him "the ruler of this world." Therefore, it shouldn't be surprising to us to see Satan using his legal authority to orchestrate destruction. There will come a point when God's Kingdom is fully restored; and when that happens, God's will shall be done perfectly on earth. In the meantime, so great is God's love for us that, rather than letting us live with the consequences of our rebellious act, He himself took on the punishment to restore all creation to His original intent. We can experience the benefits of God's Kingdom now, albeit not fully yet.[48] We will discuss this in the next chapter.

But not everything that happens is a result of Satan's direct attack. We must also acknowledge that much of the brokenness we experience is the result of the exercise of our free will.

The Exercise of Our Free Will

In the last chapter we established that humans are the only created beings that have the capacity to receive God's love and love Him in return; but we aren't obligated to do so. Love isn't love unless it's freely given. So, because God wanted creatures with whom He could share His love, He created us as free-will agents. This means we can choose whether or not to live in relationship with God; and we can choose whether to live according to God's will—His wishes and desires, as well as His counsel or advice. Whenever we use our free will to go against God's will, we suffer the consequences. Hear Jesus lamenting over Jerusalem and their refusal to accept God's will:

"O Jerusalem, Jerusalem, the city that kills the prophets and stones those who are sent to it! How often would I have gathered your children together as a hen gathers her brood under her wings, and you were not willing!"

Matthew 23:37

Because we have free will, the Father won't impose His will on us. He longs to love us and show us how to live in fullness of life; but He respects our wishes and allows us to make our choices, even if those are against His will. Then, we reap the consequences of our own choices. If we choose to go against God's will, we may experience brokenness as a result. He teaches us how to live and when we obey, our lives are preserved; but when we violate His instruction, we can't say that He is the author of the ensuing destruction.

Let me give you an example. I have a niece—Natalia—who loves to spend time at our home. When she was younger, every time she came over she wanted scrambled eggs and avocado. (Perhaps that is an indication of my cooking skills). Being the good aunt I am, I was always happy to oblige.

On one occasion, when she was about five, she was feeling quite "grown up" and asked if she could scramble her own eggs. I was happy to let her help and eager for her to learn, so I set up a chair by the stove and gave her clear instructions not to touch the stove at all. I showed her our glass-top burner, pointed to the fiery glow, and said, "If you touch this, it will burn you. Do not touch!" She followed my instructions. Well … almost.

As soon as I turned the burner off and removed the skillet, she put her little hand on the hot surface and immediately screamed in pain. The blisters started forming right away. Kerry and I did what a loving aunt and uncle would do: took her in our arms, put burn cream on her hand, bound up her wound, and comforted her. We reassured her we weren't upset with her and reminded her how much we loved her. She learned a valuable lesson.

Now let me ask you a few questions.

Do I think the lesson Natalia learned was valuable? Yes.

Did I take her hand and put it on the hot stovetop for her to learn a lesson? No way!

Did I cause the burn to punish her for disobeying my order? Certainly not.

Could I have kept it from happening? Of course. I could have denied her request to help, or strapped her hands to ensure she wouldn't hurt herself. But I was showing her my love by helping her grow up.

Did she feel comforted and loved when we took steps to help her? I believe she did.

But just because some good came out of it doesn't mean we wanted it to happen or we made it happen. It just means that, as loving adults, we used a bad situation to bring some good out of it.

Now let's take it further.

Did God cause the burning of Natalia's hand? Was He punishing her or wanting to harm her to teach her a lesson? I don't think so.

Did the enemy cause it? Very unlikely.

Did Natalia's free will cause it? In a sense, yes. She acted based on the knowledge she had, with few outside restrictions.

Could God have stopped it? Yes; by overriding Natalia's free will. But He is a loving God, so He won't force His will on us.

In the exercise of our free will, sometimes we make outright deliberate choices that go against God's design for us. Sometimes we take missteps, fall and hurt ourselves. We may be making the best choice with the information we have available at the time, and still experience adverse results. There is no guilt in this; no condemnation. But the Father lets us do it. It's part of His gift of freedom.

God doesn't want robots who are forced to obey Him. He wants a relationship of love, which demands freedom to accept or reject His instruction and counsel. God could override our decisions and force us to do what He says; but this would go against His purpose of developing free relationships.[49]

Because of this, it's also possible to experience brokenness as a consequence of someone else's free will. Imagine someone who gets drunk, goes on a shooting spree, and kills someone else. Could we say that this was God's will? Not at all. God tells us not to be drunk (because it's destructive); but He won't override someone's free will in the matter. He must allow it, even if the consequences are fatal.

Perhaps you have been the victim of someone else's willful disobedience to the Father's instruction. I know it's difficult to accept, and I'm sorry for your suffering. But please know that this was neither the Father's plan nor His design. If you allow Him, He wants to bind up your wounds, comfort, strengthen and affirm you. If you turn it over to Him, He can make something good out of it.

There are also things that can't be traced to either Satan's direct attack or the exercise of human free will. Some things are the result of the cumulative effect of humanity's sin. Let me explain.

The Cumulative Effect of Humanity's Sin

In Genesis 3 we read that Adam and Eve chose to eat of the Tree of the Knowledge of Good and Evil. Humans basically told God, "We can take care of ourselves. If we just have more information, we can work things out on our own." From that point, we have been mismanaging earth and its resources. God intended for us to rule the planet in partnership with Him, but we have chosen to do it on our own and have made a mess of things!

As we mentioned in chapter 1, a wrong view of God, and therefore of reality, results in separation from God, separation from ourselves, separation from each other, and separation from nature. The consequences of each of these are devastating, so we can safely say that much of the brokenness we experience in our world has its roots in a wrong view of God.

Now we live in a world where resources are scarce, so we see famine, poverty, and exploitation. We live in a polluted planet and our food supply has been altered so much that our bodies can't function as God intended. In the West we live under the burden of productivity, which produces stress resulting in all forms of illnesses. The earth has been subjected to mismanagement, which causes climate disturbances and thus, natural disasters. This was never God's design for us.

We might still wonder, since God is all-powerful, why doesn't He do something about it?

Is God Powerless to Stop Bad Things from Happening?

To answer this question, I want to ask you to think through three scenarios. There are three couples, each with a different view of parenting.

The first couple loves their child so much that they want to prevent all possible harm. As the child begins to take his first steps, they hold his hand and never let it go.

The second couple loves their child so much that they want her to learn how to walk quickly. They know the process of learning involves falling and learning how to get up. Whenever the baby takes a few steps, they knock her down expecting her to learn her lesson and develop walking skills from the proverbial "school of hard knocks."

God intended for us to rule the planet in partnership with Him.

The third couple loves their child so much that they want him to learn how to walk. They also know the process of learning involves falling and learning how to get up; so early on they hold his hand. Little by little, they give him more and more freedom. Whenever he falls, they pick him up, comfort him, and encourage him to get up and try again and again, until he learns how to walk on his own.

Let me ask you, which of these would you say is the best parenting approach? The answer should be simple. Now remember that Jesus said:

If you then, who are evil, know how to give good gifts to your children, how much more will your Father who is in heaven give good things to those who ask him!
Matthew 7:11

Our own parenting skills pale in comparison with the Father's heart toward us. But we can see through Scripture that, as a good Father, *Abba* wants us to grow up. He wants us to learn to walk on our own, to trust Him freely, and to exercise our free will responsibly. He knows in the process we may stumble and fall and even hurt ourselves—and sometimes others—but He won't curtail our free will.

Yes, God is sovereign; which basically means that He can do whatever He wants. But we must understand there are two aspects of sovereignty: *de jure* and *de facto*.

We could say that *de jure* means legal authority. It's what rightfully belongs to someone. If I am driving and come to a red light, I must stop. But once it turns green, I have *de jure* ability to go. I can legally go across the intersection if I want to.

By contrast, *de facto* refers to what is actually the case. It is factual. Using the driving example, when the light turns green, I may have *de jure* authority to go; but if there is another car stopped in front of me, I don't have *de facto* ability. Even if I wanted to do so, there is something else that prevents me from doing what I desire and can rightfully do.

Applied to God, we can say that at every moment God is completely sovereign *de jure* but not necessarily *de facto*.[50] That is, though He has the authority to do whatever He wants, there may be other factors that prevent Him from actually doing it.

In God's sovereignty, He chose to create humanity as relational beings with free will, such that we can share in His love but aren't obligated to do so. This is a loving act of God. In God's sovereignty, **He is working** He chose to limit Himself to protect our free-will **to redeem and** for the purpose of relationship. This is also a loving **restore all** act of God. Therefore, in the affairs of the world **that has been** there may be many instances where He has *de jure* **broken by sin.** sovereignty to override human free will, but He won't do it—not because He is not powerful enough, but because He is too loving to revoke our free will.

Nevertheless, when the human exercise of our free will results in destruction, God's sovereignty is such that somehow He can use it for good. Whenever we face the pain of the brokenness that is present in our world, we must know that *Abba* is not passive about it. He is working to redeem and restore all that has been broken by sin. We shall see this in the next chapter.

So far, we have seen that the bad things that happen in the world aren't the Father's will. But what about good things? Surely God can do all the good that He intends to do, right? Or is it possible that there are things that God wants to do that aren't being done? Let's touch on this briefly to wrap up this chapter.

Our Partnership in God's Will

Remember from the creation account that God created us in His image and likeness with the express desire that we would share with Him in caring for His creation. God wants to partner with us.

Then God said, "Let us make man in our image, after our likeness. And let them have dominion over the fish of the sea and over the birds of the heavens and over the livestock and over all the earth and over every creeping thing that creeps on the earth."
Genesis 1:26

One key aspect of our partnership is prayer. Earlier in this chapter we saw that when Jesus taught us to pray, He said for us to ask the Father:

Your kingdom come,
your will be done,
on earth as it is in heaven.

Matthew 6:10

Jesus is teaching us to cooperate with the Father through prayer. We may not understand why; but what is clear is that "God has tied Himself irrevocably to human cooperation in the execution of divine purposes."[51] This goes back to his *de jure* and *de facto* sovereignty. God has legal authority to do whatever He wants but He has chosen to partner with humanity in the affairs of the world. Therefore, He is limited in *de facto* sovereignty to do His bidding. Said simply, there are things that God wants to do, but they don't get done except through human partnership.

Have you heard the expression, "all things work together for good?" We assume this means that God will work something good out of every situation, no matter what. But let's look at the idea in its biblical context:

Likewise the Spirit helps us in our weakness. For we do not know
what to pray for as we ought, but the Spirit himself intercedes for
us with groanings too deep for words. And he who searches hearts
knows what is the mind of the Spirit, because the Spirit intercedes for
the saints according to the will of God. And we know that for those
who love God all things work together for good, for those
who are called according to his purpose.

Romans 8:26-28

Nothing in the Bible indicates that all things work together for good, period. What this passage tells us is that human cooperation—with the help of the Holy Spirit—can impact the outcome of any situation. A better translation of verse 28 is found in the RSV and NEB translations of the Bible:

In everything God works for good with those who love Him.

Romans 8:28, RSV

In everything, as we know, [the Spirit] *cooperates for good*
with those who love God.

Romans 8:28, NEB

We have the privilege of partnering with God, in prayer and in action, to see His will established on earth. We will look at this later in our study.

Conclusion

In this chapter we have said that, even though God created a "very good" world, there are many things that happen—both in the big scheme of things and in our personal lives—that aren't good. These aren't the Father's will. Not everything that happens is God's will; and God's will is not always done on earth. Bad things happen because of (a) Satan's direct attack, (b) the exercise of our free will, or (c) because we live in a broken world and suffer the effects of the cumulative effect to humanity's sin.

Even though God is sovereign and could do something about the evil in our world, His love is such that He allows us to exercise our free will without His intervention. Said another way, in His sovereignty, God chose to limit Himself to protect our free-will for the purpose of relationship—at great cost to Himself, as we shall soon see.

Finally, we have seen that God wants for His will to be done on earth but has chosen to limit Himself to human cooperation, so we have the privilege of partnering with God—in prayer and action—for His will to be established on earth. We will come to that in later chapters. For now, we must understand that *Abba* is not passive about the brokenness in the world. He is doing something about it. To this we turn in the next chapter.

REFLECTION

Is there any brokenness in your life? Have you thought that it was God's doing? Perhaps you have been the victim of someone else's sin; but this was neither God's will nor plan for you.

Take some time to talk to God about this situation and ask Him to lead you in prayer so He can work together with you to make something good come out of it.

Have you experienced any brokenness because of your own free-will choices? Did you think the consequences were God's punishment for what you did? Remember that God is not an angry, reluctant deity in need of appeasement but a zealous lover yearning for restored relationship with His creation. Could it be that the brokenness you experienced was not God's punishment but the natural consequence of your actions?

Take some time to talk to God about this situation and ask Him to lead you in prayer so He can work together with you to make something good come out of it.

PRAYER

Father, I thank You that You have given us free will, even if this means Your will is not always done on earth. Forgive me for the times I have blamed You for the bad things that were happening, where I didn't have understanding. Show me how to see things clearly—to discern when I am under attack, or when I am suffering the consequences of my own bad decisions. Forgive me for the times I have gone against Your will for my life, and teach me how to partner with You to turn them around for good. Where I have been the victim of someone else's sin, give me the grace to forgive them and keep my heart pure and free from bitterness or resentment. In all these things I want to partner with You to say, "Your Kingdom come, and Your will be done on earth as it is in heaven." In Jesus' name. Amen.

GROUP DISCUSSION

1. Have you heard people refer to hurricanes, tornadoes, earthquakes, or the like as "acts of God?" Discuss the implication of seeing these destructive events as acts of God. What happens to our faith when we see God as both creator and destroyer of His creation?

2. Can you think of situations where you experienced adverse consequences as a result of your own free-will choices? What can you learn from that experience?

3. Based on what we covered in this chapter can you think of ways to explain to someone else the fact that God loves us so much that He allows bad things to happen?

Five

The Father's Mission

The Father didn't send Me into the world to condemn the world,
but that the world might be saved through Me.

Jesus

"Mr. Blackman is shattered!" This phrase will go down as one of the most memorable events in my family's history. "Mr. Blackman" is the name of my father's prized family heirloom. It's a statue of a troubadour that sits atop a marble pillar, named after Count Blackman, who gave it as a gift to his beloved piano teacher. She in turn gave it to my grandmother (in gratitude for her care during a long illness), and my grandmother gave it to my parents as a wedding gift. Needless to say, the statue holds emotional significance and is always displayed in a prominent place in my father's house.

For some reason, my sister Carolina thought it would be a good idea to jump rope in the living room, right next to Mr. Blackman. As could be anticipated, the rope got tangled on Mr. Blackman's guitar, which sent him hurling down, crash-landing on the floor. It wasn't a pretty sight. There seemed to be a thousand little pieces strewn all over the living room—a devastating event (relatively speaking).

What was my father to do? One option was to accept the loss; after all, it's just a statue. Surely it could have been replaced with something else. But this was no ordinary statue. Something had to be done, so he picked up all the pieces and took it to a master restorer who carefully reassembled Mr. Blackman, leaving only microscopic traces of its earlier ruin. Mr. Blackman now sits again, atop his pillar, in my father's living room.

In much the same way—but on an infinitely larger scale—the Father is not content to discard His broken creation, count it as a loss, and move on. Remember when God created everything, He declared it was *very good*. God loves everything He created, even when the exercise of

73

humanity's free will has brought about consequences that are contrary to His original design. Creation is broken, but God isn't done with it. He created out of love, and love doesn't walk away when the beloved is in chaos. On the contrary, Jesus shows us the heart of the Father is to restore all that was created "very good" but has been marred by sin. We will explore sin as a relational issue in the next chapter. For now, we want to see the Father's mission—the essence of salvation. We start this journey by exploring how the Father responds to the brokenness in the world, as exemplified in Victor Hugo's *Les Misérables*.

Broken Creation

One of the main characters of this literary classic is Fantine—a young woman, a prostitute. Many of us, looking at her life from a Roman perspective, would say that she has "missed the mark." We say, "Fantine is a prostitute. She is a sinner. She needs forgiveness." Granted, that is important. But is that all she needs? Would God be content with forgiving her sin and yet leaving her in the condition that led to her actions? Could God look down on Fantine and say, "except for the fact that she is a prostitute, her life is very good"? You see, Fantine's story goes deeper than her actions. In fact, it's a perfect representation of the brokenness of creation, which was never the Father's desire.

Hers is the tragic story of a young woman—probably an orphan—whose lover abandons her and their young daughter, Cosette. Fantine has no option but to leave her young child in the care of some innkeepers and send her meager earnings as a factory worker to provide for Cosette's needs. When she loses her job in the factory, Fantine's situation worsens. She finds herself living in the street with no job and no income. To support herself, she sells her jewelry, then her hair, and finally her teeth. Having exhausted all other options, she reluctantly ends up selling her body. Her actions clearly aren't God's will; but neither were any of the circumstances that contributed to this outcome. We could say that Fantine's life is a picture of humanity's condition. Her life—and ours as well—is a composite of the effect of humanity's rebellion, going all the way back to the Garden of Eden.

As we saw in the last chapter, God created us as free-will agents and gave us a choice to accept His love and live in relationship with

God, or refuse it and live independently from Him. Because we have this freedom, we can choose to live according to God's will or manage our lives in our own understanding. All through the Bible we see that God gives us choices and calls for us to choose life. For example, God says:

God gives us choices and calls for us to choose life.

> *"I have set before you life and death, blessing and curse. Therefore choose life."*
>
> Deuteronomy 30:19

God wants us to respond to His love and choose life; but He won't impose it on us. This freedom is problematic, but it's God's loving act that protects our free will. In humanity's desire to have sovereignty over our own lives we make wrong choices—sometimes inadvertently, sometimes out of ignorance, sometimes with good intentions, sometimes in willful rebellion. Whatever the case may be, whenever we use the gift of free will to reject God's plans and counsel, we suffer the consequences. These choices result in the destruction of God's creation.

From a Roman, legal perspective, God has every "right" to look upon us and say, "You have made a mess of my creation. Someone has to pay!" If we approach our relationship with God through this Roman lens, we assume that Jesus' work of salvation is all about forgiving us for our bad behavior. In Fantine's example, she needs forgiveness for her actions; and of course, in His mercy, God does offer forgiveness through Jesus for everything that she does against His will. This applies to all of us. But to understand fully the Father's mission, we must look at it through the perspective that Jesus gives us of God as a Father who looks upon the entirety of the brokenness and longs to make us whole.

The Essence of Salvation

Jesus reveals that *Abba* is concerned with wholeness, not judgment. He is intent on gathering the million fragments of shattered creation and restoring it back to His original design. For every time we have chosen death, the Father doesn't look for a guilty party to judge and condemn; instead, *Abba* offers the possibility of restoration. Lest we be confused on

Salvation is much more than forgiveness of our bad behavior. the matter, Jesus states it specifically in His encounter with Nicodemus. Jesus says of Himself:

> *For God did not send his Son into the world*
> *to condemn the world, but in order that the world*
> *might be saved through him.*
>
> John 3:17

We need to emphasize this because many of us have a view of a God who sets up demands from His creatures and is looking to condemn and punish us. But notice that verse 17 says that *"God did not send his Son into the world to condemn the world."* As Eugene Peterson describes it:

> *God didn't go to all the trouble of sending his Son merely to point*
> *an accusing finger, telling the world how bad it was.*
> *He came to help, to put the world right again.*
>
> John 3:17, MSG

We could say that, through Jesus, God didn't condemn the world because He forgives our bad behavior. Again, that is Roman thinking, which falls short of describing God's intent. We need a greater understanding of what He means when He says that God sent Jesus "in order that the world might be saved through him." Salvation is much more than forgiveness of our bad behavior. To help us understand what Jesus is saying, we need to look at the original language of this verse.

The Greek word translated save is *sōzō*, which has a broad meaning including, "to save, to keep safe and sound, to save one suffering from disease, to make well, heal, or restore to health; to rescue or preserve one who is in danger of destruction."[52] The sense is that salvation encompasses the entirety of life. It's both preventive and restorative, rescuing from destruction and making someone whole. The same sense is found in the Hebrew text. In one of the many prophecies of Isaiah about the promised Messiah (Jesus), we find the equivalent concept:

> *I will make you as a light for the nations,*
> *that my salvation may reach to the end of the earth.*
>
> Isaiah 49:6b

The Hebrew word translated salvation is *Yeshua*, which means "salvation, deliverance, health, welfare, prosperity, and victory."[53]

Given these definitions, we can surmise that salvation is much more than forgiveness of sins. Salvation involves protection, deliverance, and restoration. It is the Father's act of taking all the shattered pieces of His broken creation and putting them back together. Let's take it further by looking at the prophetic descriptions of Jesus' mission.

Characteristics of Jesus' Mission

In the Gospel of Matthew, we see a reference to one of the many prophecies about Jesus, the Messiah:

> *Behold, my servant whom I have chosen,*
> *my beloved with whom my soul is well pleased.*
> *I will put my Spirit upon him,*
> *and he will proclaim justice to the Gentiles.*
> *He will not quarrel or cry aloud,*
> *nor will anyone hear his voice in the streets;*
> *a bruised reed he will not break,*
> *and a smoldering wick he will not quench,*
> *until he brings justice to victory;*
> *and in his name the Gentiles will hope.*
> Matthew 12:18-21

The Father starts by speaking of Jesus and how much He delights in Him. Then we see the work of the Holy Spirit—again, a picture of the Trinity working together on behalf of humanity. The picture that we see here is not that of a strict, punishing Father; but a loving, tender God who identifies with our weakness. When He sees that we are bruised, He won't break us. When He sees that our light is dim, He won't be the one snuffing it out. On the contrary, Jesus came to proclaim justice—the hope of a better kingdom and a better future. Look at what Isaiah prophesied about Jesus:

> *Surely he has borne our griefs and carried our sorrows;*
> *yet we esteemed him stricken,*

> *smitten by God, and afflicted.*
> *But he was pierced for our transgressions;*
> *he was crushed for our iniquities;*
> *upon him was the chastisement that brought us peace,*
> *and with his wounds we are healed.*
> *All we like sheep have gone astray;*
> *we have turned—every one—to his own way;*
> *and the Lord has laid on him*
> *the iniquity of us all.*
>
> Isaiah 53:4-6

Here we see that Jesus bore all the consequences of our sin in order to make us whole. What He did (and still does) goes much farther than simply forgiving our offenses. He doesn't just take the punishment we deserve, but also restores our peace and heals us. Because we have gone astray, choosing to live independently from our Creator, we had no hope; but Jesus takes on Himself all of humanity's brokenness to make us whole. Jesus restores our hope. In Luke's Gospel, we see where Jesus takes the scroll of Isaiah and reads about Himself:

> *The Spirit of the Lord is on me,*
> *because he has anointed me*
> *to proclaim good news to the poor.*
> *He has sent me to proclaim liberty to the captives*
> *and recovering of sight to the blind,*
> *to set at liberty those who are oppressed,*
> *to proclaim the year of the Lord's favor.*
>
> Luke 4:18-19

Notice the many facets of Jesus' mission. He preaches good news to the poor and proclaims freedom for the prisoners. There is hope! He brings recovery of sight for the blind. There is healing! He releases the oppressed. There is deliverance! And He proclaims the year of the Lord's favor. God is for us! Jesus comes to give us good news about the Father—not bad news. Jesus comes to save humanity, not just from Hell, but from anything and everything not whole as *Abba* intended it to be.

What He did (and still does) goes much farther than simply forgiving our offenses.

From the prophetic descriptions of Jesus' ministry we see that the Father is committed to making you whole. He is committed to healing, to restoring anything in you that has been broken by sin. For what purpose? Why does He want you whole? Why would God go to such great lengths to save you? Because He wants you to experience eternal life. Let's explore what that means.

The Promise of Eternal Life

Let's go back to John 3 and Jesus' conversation with Nicodemus. Here we find one of the best-known verses in Scripture—a clear reference to the Father's mission. Jesus speaks of eternal life, revealing the Father's motivation, His method, and His intent:

> *For God so loved the world, that he gave his only Son,*
> *that whoever believes in him should not perish but have eternal*
> *life. For God did not send his Son into the world to condemn the*
> *world, but in order that the world might be saved through him.*
> John 3:16-17

"God so loved the world." This is His motivation. God created out of love and He continues to love even though the use of our free will has made a mess of things. The world is not as it should or could be; it has been broken by sin. But God loves the world; so, as we said earlier, God doesn't just sit passively lamenting the current state of affairs. Instead, He took it upon Himself to do something about it. What did He do?

"He gave his one and only Son." This is His method. God could have sent us an instruction manual. He could have sent angels or raised up leaders or guides. He had unlimited options at His disposal. But because God is infinite, overflowing, outgoing, self-giving love, God gives of Himself. Therefore, in the most incomprehensible, earth-shattering event in history, God put on human flesh. Jesus was born of a virgin, by the Holy Spirit. He is fully God and fully man. Through the incarnation God fully identified with His creation, experiencing the fullness of the broken human condition. He took our brokenness and all the consequences of our rebellion. Jesus paid the price for our sin; but He also conquered death and secured our victory, as we shall soon see. Why did He go to such great lengths?

This is eternal life, and it has already begun. *"That whoever believes in him shall not perish but have eternal life."* This is His intent. Jesus didn't become human, die, and rise from the dead just so we can have the proverbial "ticket to Heaven." He didn't go through all of that just so we could spend eternity in heaven with Him. That is one of the many benefits we can enjoy—and I'm grateful for that promise that gives us hope! But what Jesus is saying here goes much further than that. What does Jesus mean with this phrase? The sense in the original Greek text gives us better understanding.

The tense of the phrase *"Shall not perish"* is considered without regard for past, present, or future time.[54] The tense of *"have eternal life"* is in present tense, representing a simple statement of fact or reality viewed as occurring in actual time, but that may or may not occur depending upon circumstances.[55] What this means for us is that this is not a promise reserved for a future time (after our earthly body dies), but a present, ongoing reality that we can experience in the here and now, as long as we meet the condition of believing in Jesus. In other words, because of what Jesus has done on our behalf, we don't have to remain in a state of perishing, but we can experience fullness of life. Yes! Even amid brokenness, even when circumstances are adverse, even when everything around us seems to be crumbling, we can experience life in the fullest sense of the word. This is eternal life, and it has already begun.

"Eternal life" doesn't refer to quantity of life, but to its quality. The Greek word translated eternal is *aiōnios*, which refers to that which always has been and always will be—in other words, God himself. The word translated *life* is the Greek word *zōē*, which refers to the absolute fullness of life which belongs to God. It is life real and genuine, active and vigorous—life as the Father, Son, and Holy Spirit have in themselves.[56] What does this absolute fullness of life look like?

Remember from Chapter 2 that the shared life of the Father, Son, and Holy Spirit is characterized by perfect union and harmony, abundance of love, joy, peace, affirmation, and acceptance. It is a life of perfect wholeness. When Jesus prays for us, He expresses His desire for us to experience the fullness of what it means to be human, made in the image of God and living in perfect relationship with Him—and by extension, with one another—according to His original design. This is the kind of life Jesus makes available to us, in the here and now. So great is the Father's love for us!

Finally, later in John's Gospel, Jesus summarizes His mission saying:

I came that they may have life and have it abundantly.

John 10:10b

We can share in the life of God, let His life flow from us, and live with an acute sense of purpose, significance, and worth.

Once again, the Greek word translated *life* is *zōē*, and refers to absolute fullness of life—life as God has it. Jesus plainly says this is why He came: that we may have life in the fullest sense of the word. Furthermore, He says that He came so we can have life more abundantly. This is the Greek word *perissos*, which means, "exceeding abundantly, supremely, something further, more, much more than all, superior, extraordinary, surpassing, uncommon."[57] This is not a guarantee of a trouble-free life, nor of material prosperity; it's rather a promise that, even in adverse circumstances, we can share in the life of God, let His life flow from us, and live with an acute sense of purpose, significance, and worth.

Eternal life is fullness of life; an inclusion in the life of the Trinity. It boils down to fellowship in the fullest sense of the word. God created us for fellowship with Himself, so He's not content to see the brokenness that keeps us away from Him. So great is the Father's love for us; so great is His commitment to us, that He became one of us and paid the ultimate sacrifice to reverse all the consequences of sin and restore us to fullness of life. And He does this willingly and freely. This is grace. God has committed Himself forever to the human cause, making us whole and bringing us back to fellowship with Himself. This is the essence of salvation; this is the essence of eternal life, and this is the Father's mission. Karl Barth summarizes this by stating:

In His free grace, God is for humanity in every respect. God is with us as our Creator, who intended and made us to be very good. Despite our sin, God is with us, through Jesus Christ reconciling the world and drawing us unto Himself in merciful judgment. God doesn't just cross off our past as if it was irrelevant; instead, He takes it under His care, restoring, rebuilding, and making things new. God meets us as redeemer and perfecter, beckoning from the future to show us the fullness of life that He intended from the beginning and that He is fulfilling through Christ.[58]

We cannot earn salvation, so it's no use striving for it. All we can do is receive God's gracious gift, already fulfilled in Jesus. *Abba* says to us, once again, "I have set before you life and death, blessing and curse. Therefore, choose life."

Conclusion

In the last chapter we saw that the brokenness we see around us is not the Father's will; but creation is broken, nonetheless. In this chapter we have said that the Father wants to restore broken Creation back to His original intent. To understand salvation, we must first understand that "sin" goes much deeper than simply bad behavior. In fact, as we will see in the next two chapters, destructive behavior is often a symptom of a deeper problem, and the Father is not content to leave us in our brokenness. He has done something about it!

Jesus establishes clearly that *Abba* is not intent on condemning the world, but on saving it. This means that God wants to protect, deliver, and restore us. Jesus' mission clearly shows a loving, tender God who identifies with our weakness and gives us hope. He loves us so much that He became one of us—the incarnate Son: Jesus—to set us free from the destructive patterns of our world.

Jesus bore all the consequences of our sin, once and for all, to make us whole—whole in our being, whole in our relationship with Him, and whole in our relationships with one another. By believing in Him, we don't have to live a perishing, broken existence; instead we can experience fullness of life as the Father, Son, and Holy Spirit have it. This is eternal life: the God kind of life, characterized by perfect union and harmony, abundance of love, joy, peace, affirmation, and acceptance. This is the kind of life that Jesus makes available to us—in the here and now. This is the Father's mission, and it's good news!

This is the essence of the Gospel, and God invites us to partake of His free gift. He wants us to live in the wholeness that He has made possible for us. God calls us to live holy lives. We address this in the next chapter.

REFLECTION

Have you considered the extent of God's love for you? Perhaps your life looks nothing like the very good God declared it to be when He created you. Perhaps your heart is shattered, or your circumstances are in shambles. Can you accept that the Father isn't pleased with the brokenness, but neither is He intent on condemning you? He wants to make you whole. Talk to Him about your situation. Ask Him to tell you what He sees, and how He wants to restore you.

Have you considered that *salvation* is far more than forgiveness for your bad behavior; and far more than a ticket to Heaven? Have you talked to God about areas in your life that need *salvation*? Ask Him where He sees brokenness that He wants to heal. Maybe it's a health issue; maybe it's a relationship; maybe it's emotional; maybe it's mental. Whatever it may be, Jesus already took upon Himself all your brokenness so you can be made whole.

PRAYER

Father, I thank You for Your love for us. I thank You for the way that You have given of Yourself to make us whole. I ask You to show me any area of my life that is broken, that You want to touch. Show me if there is any area that I'm holding back from You. Show me if there is any area in which I'm holding on to brokenness. Lord, I open my life to You. I ask You to come, to touch my heart, make me whole, make me clean, and bring me back into fellowship with You. I want to experience eternal life. I want to experience life to the fullest—life as You have it. Father, I thank You for salvation. Thank You for sending Jesus, Your Son, to take all our sin and its consequences to make us whole. Jesus, I receive You again into my life. I receive You and everything You are. I receive the Holy Spirit into my life to transform me from the inside-out. I give You my heart, and I give You permission to restore me. I thank You for who You are, and for Your great, amazing love for us. In Jesus' name. Amen.

GROUP DISCUSSION

1. What is the meaning of "salvation" and why is it important for us to know that it's more than "a ticket to Heaven"?

2. Based on the Scriptures discussed in this chapter how would you explain the Father's mission to someone else?

3. A frequent question in the Church is whether someone can lose his/her salvation. Based on what we have seen of the Father's mission, how would you respond to that?

Six

The Father and Holiness

Be perfect, therefore, as your heavenly Father is perfect.
—Jesus

Kerry tells a story of traveling to speak at a leadership conference in France. After almost missing the train, he settled in his seat ready for the three-hour ride from Paris to Vichy, France, only to realize something was wrong with his ticket. Because Kerry doesn't speak French, he relied on the kindness of strangers to point him from platform to platform until he finally found the right train. Now the man on the seat next to his was pointing to Kerry's ticket saying, *"Première, première!"* Kerry hadn't realized that his travel agent had secured first class tickets for him. Grateful that this stranger had the boldness to share this information, Kerry picked up his luggage and made his way through several cars until he reached the first-class car, where a comfortable seat with food and beverages had been reserved for him. After a couple of hours, they reached their destination. Kerry would have arrived to Vichy either way—whether riding in a first- or third-class car; but the journey was much more pleasant when he enjoyed all the benefits that his ticket provided for him.

In much the same way, when we think of salvation in terms of our eternal destination, all we need to do is trust in Jesus, and receive Him as Lord and Savior. We have the "ticket" to Heaven. However, as we saw in the last chapter, there is much more to salvation than just our destination. Jesus has provided *eternal life* for us. He has made a way for us to enjoy fullness of life, but we have a part to play in this. The key to experiencing *eternal life* in the here and now is holiness. Because *Abba* wants the best for us, He wants us to have abundant life, so He calls us to be holy as the Father, Son, and Holy Spirit are holy.

Chiqui Wood

Called to Holiness

In Leviticus 11:44 God says to the Israelites, "Be holy, for I am holy."
He reminds them that He is their God, and again calls them to holiness:

*For I am the Lord who brought you up out of the land of Egypt
to be your God. You shall therefore be holy, for I am holy.*
Leviticus 11:45

And once again:

*Speak to all the congregation of the people of Israel and say to
them, You shall be holy, for I the Lord your God am holy.*
Leviticus 19:2

God called Israel to be set apart—to be separate from the
surrounding nations. He repeatedly called them to Himself; to live in
relationship with their God so they wouldn't have to act like the pagans
around them. We see in the New Testament that God calls us, even
today, to live holy lives:

*As obedient children, do not be conformed to the passions of your
former ignorance, but as he who called you is holy, you also be
holy in all your conduct, since it is written,
"You shall be holy, for I am holy."*
1 Peter 1:14-16

When you hear those verses, what picture comes to mind? For
many of us, the image that we see is that of a judge pointing a long
finger and saying, "Shape up or else." If we think this way, it's because
we misunderstand both the problem of sin and the essence of holiness.
God calls us to be holy, as He is holy; but we miss the mark. We sin. The
problem, however, is not the behavior itself. We need a right perspective
of sin before we can embrace God's call to holiness.

The Problem of Sin

For most of the Western Church, our thoughts regarding sin have been formed in a Roman, legal context.[59] We say that sin is breaking the Law, or "missing the mark." We focus on behavior and measure it against what we know to be God's will. If it doesn't match up,

Rather than trusting God's love to protect and provide for them, they began looking for ways to protect themselves.

we call it "sin." However, as described in chapter 1, the Roman view is an incomplete, distorted perception of reality. The meaning of "sin" in the Hebrew worldview is the loss or injury of relationship. Simply put, sin is the condition of having a broken relationship with God.[60] It's separation from God, which yields brokenness. "Bad behavior" or sinful actions, are merely the symptoms of the brokenness that results from our broken relationship with God. Let me explain how this plays out.

As we said in chapter 1, a wrong view of God causes a separation between God and His creatures. We were created to live in intimate relationship with Father, Son, and Holy Spirit; but when this relationship is broken, everything else is negatively impacted. This problem goes all the way back to the Garden of Eden. We read in Genesis how Adam and Eve ate from the Tree of the Knowledge of Good and Evil. In doing so, they created a separation between them and God. They set their hearts on something other than God to be their source of knowledge, wisdom, protection, and provision. In doing so, they felt shame; they were afraid; they hid and covered themselves. Rather than trusting God's love to protect and provide for them, they began looking for ways to protect themselves and restore what they had lost. They began blaming each other (and even God), and acting in self-preservation. This story is repeated time and time again in human history. When we are separated from God, we have a tendency to look after our own interests. This separation from God, which results in self-sufficiency and self-centeredness, is the essence of sin.[61]

Jesus explains that what defiles us is not what we do, but the condition of our heart that motivates our actions:

> *What comes out of a person is what defiles him. For from within,*
> *out of the heart of man, come evil thoughts, sexual immorality,*
> *theft, murder, adultery, coveting, wickedness, deceit, sensuality,*

Do you think God is holy because He keeps a long list of do's and don'ts?

envy, slander, pride, foolishness.
All these evil things come from within,
and they defile a person.

Mark 7:20-23

When we live in self-preservation mode, we end up acting in ways that ultimately hurt us. For example, we self-medicate and become dependent on (and sometimes addicted to) things to try to hide the pain. For some people it's drugs; for others it may be alcohol or food, promiscuity or pornography. We live in fear of lack, so we do whatever it takes to secure for ourselves the things that we think we need. We lie, cheat, or steal in order to self-protect. Because we don't trust God's love, we think we need to look out for ourselves, and will do anything to ensure that we get our way. All these behaviors are the result of sin. These sinful actions hurt us and our relationships. In doing so, they rob us from experiencing the fullness of life that God desires for us.

The Hebrew lens shows us that God is not primarily concerned with right or wrong behavior, but with wholeness in relationships. It's not that our behavior is irrelevant to the Father. It matters—and it matters a lot! There are behaviors that lead to life, and there are some that lead to death. What good father would allow his child to step off a cliff? What good father would let his child play in the street? Since *Abba* is a good Father, He cares about our behavior, but not for His benefit. He teaches us the way that leads to life and warns us of the ways that lead to death. But this is for our benefit, not His. God doesn't lose His being based on anything that we do. He doesn't need our performance for Him to be God. He doesn't need us to be good so He can love us, as if He would lose anything by us not being good. But He does want us to choose life. He wants for His children to live in holiness because holiness is the key to experiencing abundant life.

When God tells us "Be holy as I am holy," He's not commanding us to control our behavior. It's more of an invitation. The picture that Jesus paints is one of a Father who looks lovingly into our eyes saying, "Come to me; I want to make you holy, even as I am holy." We will come back to this later in this chapter. Before we get there, however, we need to explore God's holiness, as it will give us understanding to what holiness means for us.

God's Holiness

When considering holiness from our perspective, we often think that holiness consists in dotting all the "I's," and crossing all the "T's." We think holiness is the practice of observing a long list of do's and don'ts. When this is the case, we focus on building external restraints and developing our character and willpower. We measure and judge one another based on what we consider to be "good behavior." But I want you to remember that God calls us to be holy, as *He is holy*. Do you think God is holy because He keeps a long list of do's and don'ts? Does God go about exercising His willpower to do certain things and abstain from doing others? Of course not! We must consider what it means for God to be holy, in light of who He is. Only then can we understand what it means for us to be holy as *He* is holy.

God's holiness can be understood in three dimensions. First, God is holy in that *He is unique among, or set apart from all other gods*. There is no god like our God who is Three-in-One, relational in His being. God is love, and there is no other god like Him. All other gods are self-serving and have no relationship with humanity, except for expecting humans to appease them through works and worship; but our God is other-centered, loving, merciful, and just. He is unique, unlike any other god. As such, God is holy. Clearly, this aspect of God's holiness doesn't apply to us.

God is also holy in that *He is different from creation*. He is beyond the world He has made. As God explains through the prophet Isaiah:

> *For my thoughts are not your thoughts,*
> *neither are your ways my ways, declares the Lord.*
> *For as the heavens are higher than the earth,*
> *so are my ways higher than your ways*
> *and my thoughts than your thoughts.*
>
> Isaiah 55:8-9

Many times, we unconsciously think of God as being a much better version of humanity, but He's not just a super-human; He is wholly other. He is the Creator, not the created. He sustains the universe by the strength of His might. He is sovereign over all of creation. As such, God is holy. Again, this aspect of God's holiness doesn't apply to us.

> **Abba relates to you from unconditional self-giving love, not on the basis of what you do but on the basis of His love for you.**

Finally, God is holy in that *He is just and totally righteous in all that He does.* God is always fair with His creatures.[62] We could appropriately say that He behaves rightly and justly. It's in this sense that we are called to be holy as He is holy. However, we must understand that God's holiness goes much deeper than behavior. God doesn't just choose to *do* good. Everything He does *is* good because goodness is His nature.

The Father, Son, and Holy Spirit exist in a perfect relationship of love. As such, God is whole in His being. God lacks nothing. He doesn't have to self-protect. God doesn't operate in self-preservation. Everything God does is other-centered. All of His actions flow from His wholeness.

We understand that the predominant characteristic of God's way of being is not holiness but love. In other words, understanding God as first and foremost relational, we could spell holiness as "w-h-o-l-e-n-e-s-s." Holiness is an expression—a natural outflow—of His way of being as a relational God who is love. We can't separate the two.

God is holy because He is love; and in keeping with holiness, God's love is unconditional. It's important for us to know this, or we will misunderstand why and how He calls us to be holy. Let's look at God's love as it applies to holiness.

God's Unconditional Love

As we have seen in earlier chapters, God is by nature infinite, other-centered, self-giving, overflowing love. God created everything out of love; He sustains the world through love, and He's on a mission of restoring the world because He loves His creation. Because He created you out of love, He loves you and considers you to be *very good. Abba* relates to you from unconditional self-giving love, not on the basis of what you do but on the basis of His love for you. Scripture is clear about this:

> *God shows his love for us in that while*
> *we were still sinners, Christ died for us.*
>
> Romans 5:8

Jesus' loving act of redemption makes it clear that God didn't wait for us to get it all together. He didn't wait for us to clean up our act; He didn't wait for us to walk straight and fix our own brokenness before He could love us. No! He loved us first, and still loves us. In Brennan Manning's famous words, "*Abba* loves each of us just as we are, regardless of whether we ever change one thing about ourselves. He loves us as we are, not as we should, could or would be."[63]

Abba is never repulsed by your behavior, and He will never reject you based on what you do.

Know this: *Abba* is never repulsed by your behavior, and He will never reject you based on what you do. You didn't do anything to deserve God's love; and you can't do anything to keep Him from loving you. Our sin doesn't separate us from God. Rather, it's separation from God that is the essence of sin. But Jesus comes to restore us to the Father and, in doing so, to make us whole. (Just to be clear, I'm not advocating universalism. Because we have free will we can reject God and His ways. This rejection has consequences now and for eternity; but the root of the problem is not behavior, but refusal to be in restored relationship with God.) As mentioned earlier, the Father wants you to be holy, not for His sake, but for yours. He is not primarily concerned with your behavior, but with your wholeness. As Max Lucado puts it, "God loves you just as you are, but too much to leave you that way." We can be assured of this by looking at Jesus' ministry.

Holiness is Wholeness

Jesus lived as a Jew in a context of strict adherence to the Law. The Pharisees studied the Scriptures daily to observe every jot and tittle of the Law. They had developed a system of over 600 laws. Their understanding was that if they observed the Law meticulously, they might be declared righteous. They thought their right standing with God was based on behavioral perfection. However, Jesus corrects their thinking:

> *You search the Scriptures because you think that in them*
> *you have eternal life; and it is they that bear witness about me,*
> *yet you refuse to come to me that you may have life.*
>
> John 5:39-40

Jesus declares that life is not found in following the letter of the Law. He himself is the giver of life, and relationship is the key. Eternal life is found not in behavior, but in relationship with Him.

According to the Pharisees' laws, they had to keep away from anything unclean lest they become contaminated and lose their holiness. But when Jesus came on the scene, He turned it all around. He didn't live by the same rules. Jesus didn't shy away from sinners. He allowed a sinful woman to anoint Him (Luke 7:39-50). He ate with tax collectors and sinners (Matthew 9:10-13). He touched lepers, and didn't become unclean (Matthew 8:1-3). On the contrary, Jesus imparted His purity to them. Jesus made them whole again. The holiness of the Pharisees was external. Jesus' holiness flowed from within and had the power to clean and restore whatever uncleanliness He encountered.

The Pharisees couldn't understand Jesus' behavior, so they accused Him. Jesus answered them by clarifying that the standard of perfection was even higher than they thought:

For I tell you, unless your righteousness exceeds that of the scribes and Pharisees, you will never enter the kingdom of heaven.
Matthew 5:20

The verses that follow show how utterly impossible it is to keep the Law: hatred is murder; lust is adultery; a change of mind is equal to breaking an oath, and so on. The hearers would have been expecting Jesus to declare full adherence to the letter of the Law, but Jesus took it further saying that it's not the letter of the Law but the spirit behind it that matters. His point was not to give us yet more rules to consider, but to show us that righteousness (right standing with God) is not a matter of behavior but a way of being that we cannot attain on our own. Then Jesus wrapped it all up saying:

You therefore must be perfect, as your heavenly Father is perfect.
Matthew 5:48

You may be thinking, "Wait a minute! This doesn't seem right. It seems that Jesus has set the bar way higher than we could ever achieve, and now He commands us to measure up!" But perhaps He is not issuing a command, but a promise. To understand what He is saying, it helps to look at the original language.

You can be whole, as your heavenly Father is whole. This is a real possibility for you. You don't have to remain in a state of brokenness.

The word translated as *perfect* is the Greek word *teleios*, which means, "Brought to its end, finished, wanting nothing necessary to completeness."[64] In this case, the word that Jesus used is translated as *perfect*, but its essential meaning is the same as the word *holy*. The English word *holy* is derived from the medieval English *hal*, which is also the root for *health, healing,* and *whole*. Both *perfect* and *holy* speak of wholeness of being, not behavior. Remember that God's actions flow from His wholeness. Because God is whole in His being, three-and-one relationality, He doesn't look to His own interests. Everything God does is other-centered. When the Father tells us to be holy as He is holy, He is calling us to a way of being that results in a wholesome way of acting.

Jesus is not setting an insurmountable standard of behavior but refuting the pattern of the Pharisees. He is making it clear that we can be holy, as God is holy, but not on our own effort. Instead of picturing God pointing His finger and saying, "Shape up or else," we can see Jesus showing us a Father who looks lovingly into your eyes saying, "You can be perfect, therefore, as I am perfect." Jesus is saying, "You can be whole, as your heavenly Father is whole. This is a real possibility for you. You don't have to remain in a state of brokenness." Jesus calls us to Himself and makes us holy.

God's Provision for Holiness

The Father wants us to be whole. He calls us to be whole, and has made a way for us to be whole. *Abba* never puts the burden on us to make ourselves whole. That would be like telling a cripple, "Walk straight!" Hard as he may try, he just can't do it. Sometimes we approach holiness this way. We create braces, give them to crippled people and say, "Put these on, and then you can walk straight." But the problem is still there. There may be an appearance of wholeness, but the condition persists. There's a deeper problem that needs to be fixed. God isn't interested in us looking whole; He wants us to be whole—and calls us to walk accordingly.

The Father doesn't set up a set of impossible expectations for us. Instead, He issues a promise. "Because I am holy, and because you are my child, holiness is a real possibility for you. As you grow in relationship with me, you will be holy as I am holy." So committed is God to our holiness, that Jesus comes to us as what the Early Church Fathers called, "the Physician of our Humanity." He is the Great Physician who makes us whole. Jesus told the Pharisees:

Those who are well have no need of a physician, but those who are sick. Go and learn what this means: "I desire mercy, and not sacrifice." For I came not to call the righteous, but sinners.
Matthew 9:12-13

Jesus is no ordinary physician. He doesn't just come, examine us, determine what is wrong, give us a prescription, and leave us to get better as we follow His instructions. No! He himself becomes the patient. Jesus became human and took on Himself all our brokenness, all our sin, and all the consequences of the many choices that we make that are contrary to the Father's will. He, who has always existed in a whole relationship with the Father, becomes one with His creation and restores the relationship so we can be made whole in relationship with God. We aren't just healed through Christ, because of the work of Christ, but in and through Christ.[65]

Being whole is a real possibility, not because of our own effort nor because of our willpower, but because Jesus himself took our brokenness to make us whole. When we receive Jesus and accept what He has done for us, the process of wholeness begins. (This process is described in greater detail in *The Abba Factor* and *The Abba Formation*.) God himself takes the initiative and gives us the Holy Spirit to change us from the inside-out. Notice the promise He made through the prophet Ezekiel:

I will sprinkle clean water on you, and you shall be clean from all your uncleannesses, and from all your idols I will cleanse you. And I will give you a new heart, and a new spirit I will put within you. And I will remove the heart of stone from your flesh and give you a heart of flesh. And I will put my Spirit within you, and cause you to walk in my statutes and be careful to obey my rules.

You shall dwell in the land that I gave to your fathers, and you
shall be my people, and I will be your God.

Ezekiel 36:25-28

Paul shows us in the New Testament how the Holy Spirit is the one who teaches us how to walk in the newness of life that we have. First, he tells us to work out our salvation:

Therefore, my beloved, as you have always obeyed, so now, not
only as in my presence but much more in my absence, work out
your own salvation with fear and trembling ....

Philippians 2:12

If we take this verse in isolation, we might think that working out our salvation is a matter of choice and willpower; but we have to look at it in context because Paul explains how this comes about:

... for it is God who works in you,
both to will and to work for his good pleasure.

Philippians 2:13

God takes the initiative and the Holy Spirit works in us to change our desires, so they conform to what the Father desires for us. Not only that, but the Holy Spirit also gives us the power to walk accordingly. When we receive Jesus and yield to Him, and as we allow the Holy Spirit to work in us, He changes us from the inside-out. God himself gives us the power to walk in the new life that Jesus has made available to us; and thus, we are no longer subject to the desires of our old, broken, dead nature. The key to walking in holiness is living by the Spirit:

But I say, walk by the Spirit, and you
will not gratify the desires of the flesh.
For the desires of the flesh are against the
Spirit, and the desires of the Spirit are
against the flesh, for these are opposed to
each other, to keep you from doing the
things you want to do. But if you are led
by the Spirit, you are not under the law.

God takes the initiative and the Holy Spirit works in us to change our desires, so they conform to what the Father desires for us.

95

> *Now the works of the flesh are evident: sexual immorality,*
> *impurity, sensuality, idolatry, sorcery, enmity, strife, jealousy, fits*
> *of anger, rivalries, dissensions, divisions, envy, drunkenness, orgies,*
> *and things like these. I warn you, as I warned you before, that*
> *those who do such things will not inherit the kingdom of God.*
> *But the fruit of the Spirit is love, joy, peace, patience, kindness,*
> *goodness, faithfulness, gentleness, self-control;*
> *against such things there is no law.*
>
> Galatians 5:16-23

Notice that Paul doesn't say, "try really hard so you will not gratify the desires of the sinful nature." He says, if you walk by the Spirit you will not be bound by these desires. If you walk by the Spirit, you will walk in holiness, bearing His fruit.

Conclusion

In this chapter we have established both that holiness is wholeness, and that the Father is not after our behavior but our wholeness. This can be clearly seen in the story where Jesus deals with a woman caught in the act of adultery. In John 8:3-11 we see that the Father is not out to condemn us for our sin. When the Pharisees bring to Him a woman caught in the act of adultery, Jesus doesn't condemn her. Of course, we know that He also says to her, "Go and sin no more." Our view of the Father impacts how we interpret that scene. How we interpret what is not said is as important— maybe more so—than what is said. Jesus says, "Go and sin no more." That's it. However, when we read the text, it's possible that subconsciously we think, "Okay, Jesus loved her unconditionally, as a sinner, because she didn't know any better. But now that she has had an encounter with Jesus, the rules of the game change." It's as though we fill in the script, and we hear Jesus saying something like this: "Go and sin no more, or else I will stop loving you. Since now you know better, I will withhold My love from you until you get your act together." What if the woman did in fact go back and fall in the same sin again? Would Jesus stop loving her? Would He love her any less?

We often apply the same standard to our lives—albeit subconsciously. Somehow, we hold a belief that Jesus loves us unconditionally ... until we meet Him. But once we give our lives to Him, things change, and His love becomes conditional. We live under the assumption that once we are His, He loves us based on our performance. We may not acknowledge **Holiness is about being whole.** it, but that's how it often plays out in real life. We think, "Okay, Jesus loved me unconditionally when I was a sinner, but now that I'm a saint, He expects me to perform a certain way, and then He will really love me." But how can the unconditional, infinite, overflowing love of God be measured in quantity?

What is at stake here is wholeness. As we have said, holiness is wholeness. The issue is not acceptance, but wholeness. God doesn't love us any more or any less based on what we do. He is infinite, overflowing, other-centered, unconditional love. He doesn't love us on the basis of our performance; and neither does He stop loving us according to our behavior. However, as we saw in the last chapter, He wants us to experience eternal life. Therefore, Jesus says to us, "Why would you hold onto brokenness? Why would you live beneath the quality of life that I have provided for you? If you insist on holding onto your brokenness, I won't love you any less but you will not experience the eternal life that I have come to give you. Come to me. I want to make you whole. And when I make you whole, you won't have to continue in your sin. When I make you whole, you can live the abundance of life—eternal life—as I have designed it for you."

Again, holiness is not about performance for the sake of pleasing God—so God can be pleased with us, so God can accept us, or so God can love us. Holiness is about being whole—coming to Him and allowing God, the physician of our humanity, to make us whole. In that wholeness, we won't have to continue in our sin. Jesus has come to heal our brokenness, so we don't have to continue in sin any more. This is the Good News! We are no longer subject to sin. We are now free from the law of sin and death, so we can experience wholeness and eternal life. We have been made alive with Christ, and the Holy Spirit himself comes alongside to help us walk in newness of life. This newness of life involves relational wholeness—a way of being with one another that reflects the way of being of the Father, Son, and Holy Spirit. We will address this subject in the next chapter.

For now, I want you to hear the Father saying, "Why would you continue living in the pattern of your old self? Why would you settle for anything less than the fullness of life that I have provided for you? Come, let Me make you whole. I want to bring you to Myself, restore you, make you whole, and then fill you with my Holy Spirit so you can walk in the fullness of holiness." This is what the Father says when He issues the invitation, "Be holy, as I am holy." It's a glorious promise, and a grand invitation. Will you receive it?

REFLECTION

Do you know the Father loves you unconditionally? What picture comes to mind when you hear God saying, "Be holy, for I am holy"? Have you ever felt like He was withholding His love from you because of something you had done (or not done)? Have you been afraid to come to Him? Consider how much He loved you while you were separated from Him. He loved you so much that He sent His only Son so you could be reconciled. God's love is far greater than you can imagine. You can come boldly into His presence. He is ready to receive you with open arms.

There, in the Father's embrace, ask Him if there are any areas where you are holding on to patterns of self-preservation. Ask Him if there are areas that He wants you to turn over to Him. Is there a particular behavior, addiction, or attitude that you struggle with? Ask the Father to show you the root and invite the Holy Spirit to come in, heal you, and change you from the inside-out.

PRAYER

Father, thank You for loving me unconditionally. Thank you for not holding my sin against me but making a way for me to be reconciled to you. I confess there are areas in my life that I haven't entrusted to You. I want to give you all of me. I open my heart to You and receive your forgiveness and Your love, which makes me whole. Search me, God, and know my heart; test me and know my anxious thoughts. See if there is any offensive way in me, and lead me in the way everlasting. Fill me with your Holy Spirit and teach me how to walk in Your ways. I give you permission to change my desires and conform them to Yours. Work in me both to will and to do of Your good pleasure.

I receive everything You have for me, and yield my life to You.
In Jesus' name. Amen.

(see Psalm 139:23-24 and Philippians 2:13)

GROUP DISCUSSION

Read the following stories in the Gospels where Jesus interacted with sinners and discuss the questions that follow.

- John 8:3-11—Woman caught in adultery
- Luke 7:39-50—Sinful woman anoints Jesus
- Matthew 9:10-13 (or Mark 2:15-17)—Jesus having dinner at a tax collector's house.

1. What was His attitude?

2. How is God's holiness expressed in Jesus' interaction with sinners?

3. If we are to be holy as He is holy, what should our attitude be toward sinners—those who are broken?

Seven

The Father and Relationships

"Love the Lord your God with all your heart and with all your
soul and with all your mind."
This is the first and greatest commandment.
And the second is like it: "Love your neighbor as yourself."
All the Law and the Prophets hang on these two commandments.
—Jesus

I never knew how painful broken relationships could be until I found myself dumbfounded over my mother-in-law's reaction against me after her son's death. She had come from Argentina to stay with us for several months—the last months of my late husband's battle with cancer. This was a challenging season in which Hannibal was in and out of the hospital, weak and in a lot of pain. Having Adelina with us was a much-welcome respite. Her presence was a blessing. I am convinced that nothing compares to a mother's care for her dying son. In those few months we cried, laughed and prayed together while taking turns trying to make Hannibal as comfortable as humanly possible.

I was confident that we shared a unique closeness because of what we had been through together—which made it all the more difficult why, on the night that Hannibal passed away, she took her things and left our house, saying only that she believed I had stopped loving Hannibal and was responsible for his death, and that she didn't want to see me again. She attended Hannibal's funeral but didn't speak to me. The pain was unbearable. Not only was I grieving my husband's death, but also had to deal with her accusation. I couldn't begin to imagine what I had done to elicit such a reaction. Every time I saw her, I felt a dagger going through my heart.

My inclination was to pray for God's vindication—after all, she was being unfair in judging me. Surely the Lord would set the record straight and reveal that I was "in the right." I expected Adelina to have a sudden change of heart and come in repentance to beg my forgiveness. I was waiting for God to work on her, and then for her to take the first step toward reconciliation. To my surprise, Jesus' words showed me something altogether different:

> *"Do good to those who hate you, bless those who curse you,*
> *pray for those who abuse you."*
>
> Luke 6:27-28

When I read this passage, I knew Jesus was calling me to not only forgive, but to bless and pray for Adelina. It was difficult; and yet I knew God wouldn't ask me to do something just to test me, to see if I would be obedient. As we have seen, God doesn't establish arbitrary rules and regulations for His benefit. Anything He tells us to do can be traced back to His way of being and desire for us to enjoy fullness of life. I will tell you the conclusion of the story with Adelina as we close this chapter; but first we want to explore the Father's view of relationships, which has a direct impact on how we relate to Him and to one another, and whether we enjoy the fullness of life He desires for us.

God's Relational Guidelines: The Ten Commandments

It should not be surprising to realize that God gives us explicit guidelines, all throughout Scripture, of how we ought to live. From His first dealings with the people of Israel He makes His intentions clear:

> *I call heaven and earth to witness against you today, that I have*
> *set before you life and death, blessing and curse.*
> *Therefore choose life, that you and your offspring may live.*
>
> Deuteronomy 30:19

"With God there are no rejections, only redirections." "Choose life," He says. God wants us to make good choices so we will experience fullness of life. However, let's be clear: God's love for us, and His desire to bless us, are unconditional. He never withholds His love from us, no matter what we do. As Wess Pinkham says, "With God there are no rejections, only redirections." I'm not saying that our behavior is not important; it is. There are things we can do that keep us from receiving His love and blessings. If we choose to live our life independently from Him, we will not enjoy the benefits of being children in His household; however, not because God is withholding them, but because of our posture of refusal. If we don't want Him, we won't enjoy what He freely gives. Therefore, we can understand that when God calls us to be holy He's not saying, "Act right or else!" but He's calling us to wholeness. He's painting a picture for us of what our lives can be when we accept His invitation to participate in the life of the Trinity. He wants us to experience fullness of life, which is only found in whole and healthy relationships—with Him and with one another. Remember that in the Hebrew worldview, sin is primarily the loss or injury of relationship. This means that we can look at all the laws God has given us through the lens of relationships. This is what the Ten Commandments (Exodus 20:1-17) are all about.

We always think of these as commands because of the subheading we see in our English translations, and because this is the way it has been taught from pulpits. However, in the original Hebrew text, they are the "Ten Words."[66] In listing them, English translations use the word shall, which is not necessarily an imperative word. It can be used to denote a command or exhortation; but it can also denote what is inevitable or seems likely to happen in the future.[67] Could it be, then, that these aren't "prescriptive" as much as they are "descriptive"? I am not suggesting this is the definitive interpretation of the original text (I leave that to Bible scholars); but I want us to consider them through a relational lens. Perhaps God is not giving us a performance burden, but rather painting a picture of what relational wholeness looks like. Think about this:

I am the Lord your God ... You shall have no other gods before me.
Exodus 20:2-3

We could take this as a warning: "Have no other gods or else ..." But perhaps it's not a warning as much as it is a promise. Notice that the Father starts by reminding the hearers who He is and the nature of the relationship they share. He is setting the context. So, we can hear Him saying between the lines, "If you know me and receive my love, you won't have any other gods. Why would you? I am *El Shaddai*, the all-sufficient one (Genesis 17:1). I am the only God you'll ever need." *Abba* is inviting us to know Him and trust Him. When we do, we shall have no other gods.

Next, we read:

> *You shall not make for yourself a carved image, or any likeness*
> *of anything that is in heaven above, or that is in the earth*
> *beneath, or that is in the water under the earth. You shall not*
> *bow down to them or serve them, for I the Lord your God am*
> *a jealous God, visiting the iniquity of the fathers on the children*
> *to the third and the fourth generation of those who hate me,*
> *but showing steadfast love to thousands of those who love me*
> *and keep my commandments.*
>
> Exodus 20:4-6

Again, we can take this as a warning, "Don't make carved images or else ..." But perhaps *Abba* is showing us what life looks like when we know Him and live in a healthy relationship with Him: "If you know me and receive My love, you will know there is no god like Me. You will not look to substitutes to receive what you need. Why would you? If you know Me, you know I take care of your every need. An idol can't love you like I love you. I delight in showing my steadfast love to you." *Abba* is inviting us to know Him and trust Him. When we do, we shall not make for ourselves carved images, nor will we bow down to any other gods.

Here is the next one:

> *You shall not take the name of the Lord your God in vain,*
> *for the Lord will not hold him guiltless who takes his name in vain.*
>
> Exodus 20:7

Using the Lord's name in vain is about claiming the benefits of the relationship without a real relationship. This is perhaps the commandment that is most misunderstood. We can take it to mean, "If you use My name in a dishonoring way, I will punish you." However, using the Lord's name in vain is about claiming the benefits of the relationship without a real relationship. It is using it for its power while ignoring the relationship through which God works on our behalf. We see an example of this in the story of the seven sons of Sceva who were trying to cast out demons saying, "I adjure you by the Jesus whom Paul proclaims ..." (Acts 19:11-16). They knew the name of Jesus had power, but they didn't know Jesus himself. They were using His name in vain, for the power is not in the name itself but in the person of Jesus. The delegated authority we have comes by virtue of our relationship with Jesus.[68] Therefore, God is saying, "If you want your guilt to be removed, come to Me and I will forgive and restore you, because I love you. This is on the basis of relationship, not on the basis of you using My name as a mantra. My name itself doesn't have the power to save; but when you call upon Me, I will save you. Don't just invoke My name; come to Me." *Abba* is inviting us to know Him and trust Him. When we do, we enjoy the benefits of His great mercy, patience, and lovingkindness.

The fourth word reads:

> *Remember the Sabbath day, to keep it holy. Six days you shall labor, and do all your work, but the seventh day is a sabbath to the Lord your God. On it you shall not do any work, you, or your son, or your daughter, your male servant, or your female servant, or your livestock, or the sojourner who is within your gates. For in six days the Lord made heaven and earth, the sea, and all that is in them, and rested on the seventh day. Therefore the Lord blessed the Sabbath day and made it holy.*
> Exodus 20:8-11

Once again, we can take this as a warning, "Don't work on the Sabbath, or else ..." But perhaps the Father is showing us a way to live. He says, "If you know Me and have a whole relationship with Me, you will not work yourself to death—but will know that I am your provider. I give you a gift, a day of rest to enjoy relationship with Me and with your community. This day of rest will be a sign to remind you that I make you holy (Ezekiel 20:12)." *Abba* is inviting us to know Him and trust Him. When we do, we can rest.

The first four "words" are vertical in nature; they describe what a life of holiness looks like in terms of our relationship with God. We don't keep the commandments in order to be rightly related; on the contrary, by being rightly related, we fulfill God's relational guidelines. The relationship comes first; the behavior is the natural result of a whole relationship.

The next six "words" are horizontal in nature, describing what whole relationships look like among fellow humans. As we shall see in the next chapter, these also are fulfilled when we are rightly related to God. For now, I simply want you to see that *Abba* paints for us a picture of a life of holiness—a life of wholeness—and it's all about relationships. Let's look briefly at the last six commandments (or "words."):

> *Honor your father and your mother, that your days may be long in the land that the Lord your God is giving you.*
> Exodus 20:12

You cannot experience fullness of life if you dishonor the people closest to you; the ones that brought you into this world. Honor your father and mother, and it will go well with you.

> *You shall not murder. You shall not commit adultery. You shall not steal. You shall not bear false witness against your neighbor. You shall not covet your neighbor's house; you shall not covet your neighbor's wife, or his male servant, or his female servant, or his ox, or his donkey, or anything that is your neighbor's.*
> Exodus 20:13-17

Why does God warn us against murder, adultery, stealing, bearing false witness and coveting? It's not the actions in and of themselves that He's against. He is warning us against anything that will hurt our relationships with one another. When we murder, the relationship is over. When there is adultery, trust is broken, which hurts the relationship. It's impossible to have a whole relationship with someone if we steal from him, or with another if we lie about her. When we covet what others have, we create a barrier of separation between them and us. All of these attitudes and behaviors hurt our relationships; and God says, "you cannot experience life when you cut yourself off from other people."

When God gives us relational guidelines—with Him and with one another—He does so in order to bring us into a life of holiness/wholeness where we can fully enjoy His blessing. (In *The Abba Factor* and *The Abba Formation* we describe the work of the Holy Spirit in greater detail. It is God himself who works in us for relational breakthroughs.) Before we look at more of God's relational guidelines, I need to address again the challenge we face in our culture: the problem of individualism. I want you to see how our individualistic lens distorts our understanding and robs us from the full life to which *Abba* calls us.

The Problem of Individualism

Why is God so adamant about the need for whole relationships? Because they reflect His way of being. As we saw in chapter 2, we have been created in God's image. One way in which we reflect His image is in our being three-part beings: spirit, soul, and body, but most importantly, we are made—in God's image—as relational beings. We can dissect our being, study our spirit, soul, and body;[69] but if we don't have healthy relationships we aren't fully human (in the *Imago Dei*).

If God's way of being is in relationship, it follows that we are made for relationship as well, making it impossible to conceive of humans as isolated, individual entities. As Rowan Williams puts it, "To be fully human is to be recreated in the image of Christ's humanity; and that humanity is the perfect human 'translation' of the relationship of the eternal Son to the eternal Father, a relationship of loving and adoring self-giving, a pouring out of life towards the Other."[70] This means that we are only fulfilled in our personhood in the context of whole and healthy relationships—both with God and with one another.[71]

We have seen how the Father desires for us to experience fullness of life—life as the Father, Son, and Holy Spirit have it. This is *perichoretic* life, which is life in relationship. Whole relationships aren't optional; they are essential to experiencing eternal life. Unfortunately, we live in a culture that values individualism (we explained its origins in chapter 3), and this ingrained value has impacted our understanding of Christian doctrine, to the detriment of relationality. The language we use—well intentioned as it may be—gets in the way of our understanding the significance of relationships.

In terms of salvation, we think it's about the individual. We use phrases like, "If you were the only person in the planet, Jesus would have died for you." While this may be true, if we understand the full meaning

Whole relationships aren't optional; they are essential to experiencing eternal life.

None of us is complete in isolation from other people. of salvation, we know we aren't fully saved in isolation from one another. We are made whole in relationship with God and restored in relationship with our fellow human beings. Only then can we experience eternal life.

In terms of forgiveness, we emphasize the need for people to repent and receive God's forgiveness, but don't necessarily give the same attention to the need to repent and be forgiven by those we have offended, or to forgive and bless those who have hurt us so the relationship can be restored. We think as long as we are OK with God, everything is fine. We think people are dispensable, so we don't do the difficult work of dealing with confrontation. It seems easier to dismiss one another and move on. But this ignores the fact that we aren't fully human except when we experience life in the context of whole relationships—both with God and with one another.

We interpret Scripture through an individualistic lens and regard discipleship as an individual pursuit of spiritual maturity. We read verses like:

> *You are complete in Him, who is the head*
> *of all principality and power …*
> Colossians 2:10, NKJV

… and interpret it to mean something like, "I am complete. Jesus and me, we have our own thing going, and I don't need anyone or anything else." But in this verse, the word *you* is plural. In Texas, we would say, "And y'all are complete in Him." In its context, Paul is addressing the group about his burden that they would be encouraged and knit together in love. He always thinks and speaks to the Body of believers, not to individuals. The implication is that we are complete in Him, as the Body of Christ. None of us is complete in isolation from other people, but only in relationship one with another.

Earlier in this letter Paul says:

> *Therefore, as you received Christ Jesus the Lord, so walk in him,*
> *rooted and built up in him and established in the faith, just as*
> *you were taught, abounding in thanksgiving.*
> Colossians 2:6-7

Lest we think that the "you" here refers to an individual, we must look to Ephesians 4, where Paul himself explains how it is that we are "built up in Him and established in the faith:"

We don't experience fullness of life without one another, and we can't grow in spiritual maturity by ourselves.

And he gave the apostles, the prophets, the evangelists, the shepherds and teachers, to equip the saints for the work of ministry, for building up the body of Christ, until we all attain to the unity of the faith and of the knowledge of the Son of God, to mature manhood, to the measure of the stature of the fullness of Christ, so that we may no longer be children ... Rather, speaking the truth in love, we are to grow up in every way into him who is the head, into Christ, from whom the whole body, joined and held together by every joint with which it is equipped, when each part is working properly, makes the body grow so that it builds itself up in love.

Ephesians 4:11-16

Note Paul's use of "the Body of Christ," and "we all." He is speaking of the whole body, not its individual parts. Rightly interpreted, we see that we don't experience fullness of salvation as individuals, we don't experience fullness of life without one another, and we can't grow in spiritual maturity by ourselves. We need one another. Whole relationships aren't optional; they are essential to experiencing eternal life.

Ben Campbell Johnson translates Jesus' famous words this way:

You are to give first priority to the Spirit dimension and setting your relationships right. When you get a proper perspective, these other things will take care of themselves.

Matthew 6:33

The priority in the Kingdom of God is relationality. Therefore, all the Law and the Prophets point to the necessity of whole and healthy relationships. Jesus said it this way:

So whatever you wish that others would do to you, do also to them, for this is the Law and the Prophets.

Matthew 7:12

Abba wants us to experience fullness of life and, contrary to our cultural notions of individualism, He teaches us that this life is only experienced in whole and healthy relationships—with Him and with one another. He shows us how to live and sends the Holy Spirit to give us power to live in the wholeness of life that Jesus secured for us.

We now turn to exploring more of God's relational guidelines, as demonstrated by Jesus and taught by New Testament writers. In the next chapter we will address how the Holy Spirit empowers us to live them out.

God's Relational Guidelines: The New Testament Version

When asked which is the great commandment in the law, Jesus answers:

*"You shall love the Lord your God with all your heart
and with all your soul and with all your mind. This is the great
and first commandment. And a second is like it: You shall love
your neighbor as yourself. On these two commandments depend
all the Law and the Prophets."*

Matthew 22:37-40

In other words, Jesus is saying, "if you want to fulfill the Ten Commandments, love God and love one another." What does this look like? Let's start by clarifying what He means by "love."

As we explored in chapter 1, our culture has been impacted by Roman and Greek worldviews. Through the Roman lens we think of love as a choice—something we do by obligation. However, if "love" is by obligation, is it really love? The Greek lens paints love as a feeling, an emotion. Hollywood movies have accentuated this notion of love that depends on "sparks" or "chemistry." But through the Hebrew lens we understand that love is neither a choice nor a feeling, but a shared life—a way of being with one another. God himself is the purest expression of love. Love is the way that the Father, Son, and Holy Spirit are with, for and toward one another; and, by extension, with, for and toward everything they have created. Paul describes love in its purest form:

*Love is patient and kind; love does not envy or boast;
it is not arrogant or rude. It does not insist on its own way;*

110

it is not irritable or resentful; it does not rejoice at wrongdoing,
but rejoices with the truth. Love bears all things, believes all
things, hopes all things, endures all things.

1 Corinthians 13:4-7

This is the love of the Father toward us. He is patient and kind with us. He is always looking to give, not to receive. He is not intent on self-aggrandizement, but becomes the lowliest of servants for the sake of humanity. God doesn't insist on His own way; He gives us free will, even if it costs Him the greatest sacrifice ever known. The Father keeps no record of wrongs. As far as the East is from the West, so far has He removed our transgressions from us (Psalm 103:12). *Abba* believes the best about us, is always on our side believing all things, hoping we will come to Him and receive His love. He is relentlessly pursuing us until we do.

As we see in this passage, the nature of love is other-centered. God expresses His love for us in many ways. Likewise, there are many ways in which we actively love one another, as described all over the Epistles:

- Wait for one another (1 Cor. 11:33). Let others have the right of way. Serve them before you serve yourself. Have care for one another.
- Consider that you are all part of the same body. Hurt with those who hurt; rejoice with those who rejoice (1 Cor. 12:25).
- Be compassionate one for another (1 Peter 3:8).
- Show hospitality to one another. Use the gifts you have to serve one another (1 Peter 4:9-10).
- Encourage one another (1 Thess. 4:18).
- Bear with one another. Forgive one another (Col. 3:13; Eph. 4:32).
- Submit to one another (Eph. 5:21; 1 Pet. 5:5).
- Bear one another's burdens (Gal. 6:2).
- Stir up one another to love and good works (Heb. 10:24).
- Confess your sins one to another and pray for one another (Jas. 5:16).
- Love one another. Outdo one another in showing honor (Rom. 12:10).
- Live in harmony with one another (Rom. 12:16).
- Do not pass judgment on one another (Rom. 14:13).

- Build one another up (1 Thess. 5:11).
- Instruct one another (Rom. 15:14).
- Welcome one another (Rom. 15:7).[72]

This is not intended to be an exhaustive list, but to give us an idea that loving one another is active. It has been said, and rightly so, that love is a verb. God calls us to be intentional about loving one another—even in costly ways—and Jesus shows us what this looks like. Let's explore a few characteristics of God's love in action.

Characteristics of Love

In John 4:1-26 we see an encounter between Jesus and a Samaritan woman, which shows us that Jesus is no respecter of persons. He neither discriminates nor condemns, but looks for ways to connect with people and is ready to give what He has to make them whole.

A woman from Samaria came to draw water.
Jesus said to her, "Give me a drink."
(For his disciples had gone away into the city to buy food.)
The Samaritan woman said to him, "How is it that you,
a Jew, ask for a drink from me, a woman of Samaria?"
(For Jews have no dealings with Samaritans.)
John 4:7-9

In speaking to this woman, Jesus was breaking all the social conventions of His day. It was neither proper for a man to speak to a woman in public, nor for a Jew to speak to a Samaritan; but Jesus was no respecter of persons.[73] When cultural norms created barriers between people, Jesus broke them. His love was not conditioned by gender, race, or culture. He didn't look for the things that would create separation, but looked instead for ways to connect with others.

He neither discriminates nor condemns, but looks for ways to connect with people.

Jesus said to her, "Go, call your husband, and come here." The woman answered him, "I have no husband." Jesus said to her,

"You are right in saying, 'I have no husband;' for you have had five husbands, and the one you now have is not your husband. What you have said is true."

John 4:16-18

No matter what your background or your past, God sees you as valuable because you are His.

Jesus didn't shy away from her because she had multiple husbands. He affirmed her truthfulness before addressing her weakness. He didn't ignore her brokenness; but neither did He condemn her. Rather than focusing on her faults, He saw her value and freely offered her the gift He had to give. He showed the unconditional love of the Father described in the parable of the lost sheep:

See that you do not despise one of these little ones. For I tell you that in heaven their angels always see the face of my Father who is in heaven. What do you think? If a man has a hundred sheep, and one of them has gone astray, does he not leave the ninety-nine on the mountains and go in search of the one that went astray? And if he finds it, truly, I say to you, he rejoices over it more than over the ninety-nine that never went astray. So it is not the will of my Father who is in heaven that one of these little ones should perish.

Matthew 18:10-14

No one is insignificant. God doesn't distribute His love based on our accomplishments, but loves everyone the same: male or female, Jew or Gentile, slave or free, rich or poor, ignorant or educated, influential or obscure. No matter what your background or your past, God sees you as valuable because you are His, and wants to lavish His love on you. Whole relationships are based on people's intrinsic value rather than external characteristics.

Another important characteristic of Jesus' love for people is His compassion, as seen all throughout the Gospels. In many of the stories that tell of Jesus doing miraculous works, the writers tell us that Jesus was "moved with compassion." The Greek word translated as *compassion* is *splagchnizomai*, which denotes a gut-wrenching feeling.[74] It's much more than just sympathy or pity, but a strong emotion that moves one to action. Jesus didn't just look at the crowds thinking to Himself, "Oh, I feel sorry for them …." No! He was so moved that He did something about it!

We are not to judge one another, for judgment is antagonistic to whole relationships. In John 11:32-35 we see that Jesus wept with Mary at Lazarus' tomb. In John 19:25-27 He entrusted His mother to John. In both instances we see Jesus identifying with the grief others were experiencing, and doing something about it. He was there, with them, in their pain. In the same way, the Father is with us in our pain. God's love is always expressed by action.

How to Love One Another

Two final aspects of love are critical to having whole relationships, so I want to elaborate on these. First, no judgment. We finished our last chapter by looking at how Jesus dealt with the woman caught in the act of adultery (John 8:3-11), and noted that Jesus didn't condemn her. If there was anyone who could have judged her, it would have been Jesus; but He looked instead for a way to restore her. The same is seen in our earlier example of the Samaritan woman (John 4:1-26). In these two instances, Jesus exemplified what He taught in the Sermon on the Mount:

> *Judge not, that you be not judged. For with the judgment you pronounce you will be judged, and with the measure you use it will be measured to you. Why do you see the speck that is in your brother's eye, but do not notice the log that is in your own eye? Or how can you say to your brother, 'Let me take the speck out of your eye,' when there is the log in your own eye? You hypocrite, first take the log out of your own eye, and then you will see clearly to take the speck out of your brother's eye.*
> Matthew 7:1-5

Jesus makes it clear that we are not to judge one another, for judgment is antagonistic to whole relationships. When we focus on the fault that we see in others, we automatically create a chasm that separates us from one another. Sometimes we judge others because we think that the key to wholeness is being "right." However, this is a clear indicator

God is more interested in you being rightly related than in you being right.

114

that we misunderstand God's unconditional love. It's Roman thinking. Let me explain.

God's perfect love is expressed in forgiveness.

Suppose you see someone acting in a way that doesn't seem "right." If you have a relationship of love and trust with the person, you will have ways to speak into his life in ways that promote wholeness. We cross this line when there is no such relationship and we take it upon ourselves to point out how they are in the "wrong." I'm talking about judging, pointing the accusing finger, and condemning others' actions. This posture doesn't lend itself to the building of relationships. On the contrary, it usually results in division. Consequently, we are relationally "wrong." Jesus didn't say that we must agree with everyone, and neither did He say that we should condone everyone's actions (there are clearly things that do not promote wholeness); but He did call us to love one another, even in our differences. Can we love one another and trust the Holy Spirit to bring conviction and change where it's needed? We could say it this way: "God is more interested in you being rightly related than in you being right."[75]

When Jesus was talking about not judging, I suppose that He had in mind one of our human weaknesses: the need to settle our conflicts by sorting out what happened, determining who is right and who is wrong. In our broken humanity, we look for ways to justify ourselves thinking that if we can prove we are "right," the conflict will be resolved. However, the road to reconciliation is never paved with facts. You probably know from experience that the approach of arguing until someone is "right" and the other is "wrong" only exacerbates the problem. Therefore, Jesus shows us a better way, which is the final and crucial aspect of love: forgiveness and blessing as the pathway for reconciliation.

The greatest expression of God's love for us is that while we were yet sinners, Christ died for us (Romans 5:8). God forgave us before we had the capacity to receive His forgiveness. Despite our rejecting Him, Jesus did not come to prove to us that we were in the "wrong." Instead, He took the initiative to forgive, and in doing so, to restore the relationship that had been broken by sin. Jesus demonstrated what forgiveness looks like on an interpersonal level:

*And when they came to the place that is called The Skull,
there they crucified him, and the criminals, one on his right
and one on his left. And Jesus said, "Father, forgive them,
for they know not what they do."*

Luke 23:33-34

Jesus didn't look for ways to punish His enemies. He always sought to forgive and restore. He had the ability to see beyond a person's actions and love them for who they are. God's perfect love is expressed in forgiveness, which makes for whole relationships. When Jesus calls us to be "perfect" as our heavenly Father is perfect, He does so in the context of loving our enemies, forgiving those who hurt us, and blessing those who curse us (Matthew 5:43-48).[76] One translation of this key verse reads:

*Therefore, just as your heavenly Father is complete in showing
love to everyone, so also you must be complete.*

Matthew 5:48, CEB

This is the way of holiness: wholeness in relationships. Jesus explains it in greatest detail:

*But I say to you who hear, Love your enemies, do good to those who
hate you, bless those who curse you, pray for those who abuse you.
To one who strikes you on the cheek, offer the other also,
and from one who takes away your cloak
do not withhold your tunic either.
Give to everyone who begs from you, and from one who takes
away your goods do not demand them back.
And as you wish that others would do to you, do so to them.
If you love those who love you, what benefit is that to you? For
even sinners love those who love them. And if you do good to
those who do good to you, what benefit is that to you? For even
sinners do the same. And if you lend to those from whom you
expect to receive, what credit is that to you? Even sinners lend
to sinners, to get back the same amount. But love your enemies,
and do good, and lend, expecting nothing in return, and your
reward will be great, and you will be sons of the Most High,*

for he is kind to the ungrateful and the evil.
Be merciful, even as your Father is merciful.

Luke 6:27-38

My Story of Reconciliation

It was with this understanding of holiness as wholeness in relationships that I faced the greatest relational challenge I have ever experienced. I started this chapter by sharing the story of the relational breakdown when my late husband passed away. My mother-in-law (at the time), Adelina, was accusing me unjustly. Several other family members followed her lead, adding to my grief. My heart wanted to pray for God's judgment on her; but Jesus reminded me of His desire for restored relationships and called me to take the initiative of forgiving and blessing her. Honestly, it was the last thing I felt like doing. The first few days were very difficult. I would pray, through tears, speaking words of forgiveness and blessing, asking God to heal her heart, minister to her needs, and surround her with His love. As time went on, the prayer seemed to flow more freely. My thoughts of her didn't have the original sting, and I knew my heart was turning toward her.

A couple of months later I knew something had changed. Adelina had returned to Argentina and still wasn't talking to me; but I felt a new sense of love for her. The more I prayed for her, the more my heart softened toward her. I knew the Holy Spirit was at work. There was no sense of judgment or condemnation, but only compassion. Her birthday was in September—four months after Hannibal's passing. There was still no communication, but I sent her a birthday card expressing my love and appreciation. By the time Christmas came around, nothing seemed to have changed, except that I heard that she had received my Christmas card and was grateful for it. I kept praying for her—forgiving and blessing.

The following March I went back to Argentina on a ministry trip. To my surprise, when I landed in Mendoza, Adelina was at the airport to welcome me. We hugged; we cried. She took my hands, kissed me, and asked me to forgive her for her attitude. She explained her struggle with grief and how she had processed it. I said I forgave her, and asked for her forgiveness for the pain I had caused her. We spent a good deal of time during that trip celebrating old memories and building new ones. I saw her a few more times when she came to Texas, and we enjoyed our time together. I am grateful that our relationship was restored and look forward to the time we'll be reunited in the Lord's presence.

I have experienced the fullness of life that comes through practicing God's relational guidelines, and this is my hope for you as well.

Conclusion

In this chapter we have seen that relationships are important to God— so much so, that He gives us relational guidelines as the way for us to "choose life." The Ten Commandments (or Ten Words) are all relational in nature. They teach us what life looks like when we are relationally whole. *Abba* is inviting us to know Him and trust Him. When we do, we shall have no other gods, we shall not make for ourselves carved images, nor will we bow down to any other gods, we shall enjoy the benefits of His great mercy, patience, and lovingkindness, and we can rest. *Abba* also paints for us a picture of relational wholeness with one another, including honoring our father and mother, and avoiding those things that hurt our relationships.

We live in a culture that values individualism, so it's important for us to emphasize God's desire for relationships. When God gives us relational guidelines—with Him and with one another—He does so in order to bring us into a life of holiness where we can fully enjoy His blessing. God is adamant about the need for whole relationships because they reflect His relational way of being. Since we are made in God's image, we are only fulfilled in our personhood in the context of whole and healthy relationships—both with God and with one another.

God's relational guidelines can be summed up in loving one another. Love is the way that the Father, Son, and Holy Spirit are with, for and toward one another, and, by extension, with, for and toward everything they have created. Through Jesus' life we see that love is expressed in manifold ways: Jesus is no respecter of persons; He neither discriminates nor condemns, but breaks through any obstacle looking for ways to bless others—to give in order to make them whole. Jesus finds and affirms value in people, loves unconditionally, and is moved with compassion. He shares others' pain. Jesus doesn't judge, but is quick to forgive and bless to bring about reconciliation. This is the way of holiness: showing love to everyone.

God calls us to be rightly related, and shows us what that looks like. Now we must ask, how do we do this? Is it a matter of willpower? Is God giving us a list of do's and don'ts? The good news is that *Abba* doesn't just teach us how to live, leaving it up to us to walk it out in our strength. No. He gives us the Holy Spirit, and His fruit in our lives leads to relational wholeness. We will address this in our next chapter.

REFLECTION

Can you identify some areas where you have struggled with God's relational guidelines? What is God saying to you through this chapter about the importance of being "rightly related?"

Are there any relationships in your life that need to be restored? Have you been wronged? If so, can you take God at His word, trust Him, and apply what Jesus taught? Forgive and bless. You may want to refer back to the Forgiveness Exercise at the end of Chapter 1 as a starting place.

PRAYER

Father, we thank You for calling us to choose life, and giving us relational guidelines so we can truly live. We ask You to give us a greater revelation of Your love and deepen our relationship with You, so we may know You better. We ask You to work in our hearts and teach us how to have whole and healthy relationships with You and with one another. Where we have broken relationships, we ask You to show us what we can do to work toward restoration. Give us the power to forgive and bless those who have hurt us. And where we have hurt others, give us the courage to ask for forgiveness. We commit our relationships to You. Fill us with Your Holy Spirit, that we might know how to live in a manner worthy of our calling. We acknowledge our weakness and ask for Your strength. In Jesus' name. Amen.

GROUP DISCUSSION

1. Select one of the stories from this chapter and discuss what we can learn about relationships from Jesus' example.

2. Discuss the relational aspect of the Ten Commandments. What stands out to you? How does this impact your understanding of God's desire for relationships?

3. Think about individualism and how it impacts our relationships. What can you do, in a culture that values individualism, to help others to value relationships?

Eight

The Father and Freedom

If the Son sets you free, you will be free indeed.

—Jesus

In Acts 16 we find a remarkable story of freedom. Paul and Silas were preaching in Philippi when a slave girl possessed with a spirit of divination started following them. Paul cast the spirit out of her. It seems this would be a good thing; but the owners of the girl were furious! Paul and Silas were beaten with rods and thrown in prison.

This doesn't sound like a story of freedom, does it? Here are two servants of God, going about doing good, and they end up in prison. This is not what we expect. When we talk about the Father and freedom, our expectation might be that *Abba* sets us free from any problem or hindrance. And yet here we see the opposite. Paul and Silas end up imprisoned and bound with chains. But that's not the end of the story.

Luke goes on to say that at midnight Paul and Silas were praying and singing to God, and the prisoners were listening to them. Suddenly there was a great earthquake, the foundations of the prison were shaken, the doors were opened, and everyone's chains were loosed. There's a great deliverance! We might think, *That's more like it! Now we see God coming through to set the captives free.* But that's still not the end of the story.

The jailer was awakened from sleep and, seeing what had happened and fearing that the prisoners had escaped, was about to take his own life. But here is the remarkable thing: Paul called with a loud voice saying, "Do yourself no harm, for we are all here." The jailer, stunned by these events, asked what he must do to be saved. The story unfolds with the jailer and his household believing in God, while Paul and Silas remained in prison until the magistrates of the city came and pleaded with them to leave.

True freedom is the freedom from self-preservation; it's freedom from the need to look after our own interests.

Paul and Silas exemplify true freedom. Their concern was not with whether they were in or out of prison, in chains or free from them. While they were preaching, they were free. When they were beaten, they were free. When they were in jail, they were praying and singing—because they were free. When the prison doors flew open, they didn't have a need to run out. They were already free. They had true freedom, which is an internal freedom.

In our cultural context, we think freedom is the absence of problems, the absence of hindrances, or the absence of confinement. We tend to celebrate freedom as the ability to do whatever we want. But true freedom is the freedom from self-preservation; it's freedom from the need to look after our own interests. It's the ability to live truthfully, honestly, and lovingly with God and with one another. It's the freedom to be other-centered; the freedom to respond to God without fear or hesitation. It's the freedom to choose life and live in holiness.

As we saw in the last chapter, God desires for us to experience wholeness of life, and this life is only found in whole and healthy relationships. This life of true freedom is a life of love that regards others as more important than ourselves. As John Macmurray says:

> The love-determined people have life in them, abundant life, and they turn towards life and fight for life against the forces of death. They are the people who are really alive, of whom it can be said that they possess eternal life as a well within them perpetually springing. They are the people who are emotionally free.[77]

When God sets us free, we are free indeed. In this freedom we experience fullness of life. Freedom is a complex subject, and many volumes have been written to address it in detail.[78] For purposes of this book, we will focus on one particular area with the greatest impact on our relationships: freedom from fear. To better understand how this comes about, we must first identify the problem; then we will see how God brings us to freedom, and finally we will see how this impacts our relationships.

The Problem of Fear

If you ask Christians which is the greatest commandment, it's quite probable they will accurately say:

> *"Love the LORD your God with all your heart, with all your soul, and with all your mind." And the second is like it: "Love your neighbor as yourself."*
>
> Matthew 22:37

But, do you know which is the most frequent commandment in the Bible? "Fear not!" God says, time and again, in different circumstances and different ways, "Fear not," "Do not be afraid."[79] Why do you suppose He needs to repeat that commandment over and over? Because for the most part, human life is carried out in a context of fear.

Let's be clear: there are different types of fear. We experience natural fear when we are facing imminent, present danger—like when we look down and see a rattlesnake a few feet away from us, when there is a fire, or when our life is otherwise threatened. This fear is legitimate and good. God has given us a sense of fear for our own safety, and we do well to heed it.

There is also the type of fear that results from the memory of a painful situation. I was in a terrible car accident in 1998 that still causes me to shudder when traffic on the freeway starts slowing down and it seems like the vehicles behind me (especially if it's an 18-wheeler) won't be able to stop in time. The memory of the accident puts my system on alert mode. This type of fear isn't necessarily bad, unless it keeps us from living in freedom. For example, if I was afraid of driving because of the memory of the accident, I would now be living in bondage to fear. God wants us to be free from this type of irrational fear.

There is yet another category of fear. We may fear being alone, being unloved, or not measuring up. We may fear failure or rejection.[80] We also experience fear of pain, suffering, poverty, and death. This is the most serious category, for it has to do with our sense of identity and worth, and with our sense of well-being. This fear can often go unrecognized, but it has a powerful impact in how our lives are carried out. This fear was never part of God's plan for humanity, but it's part and parcel of the broken condition of our world.

There is no defeat in life, unless we allow circumstances to separate us from His love. Fear is the greatest inhibitor of other-centered action, for it leads us to live on the defensive and look out for ourselves. We are created to live spontaneously, giving of ourselves to the world around us. However, a heart that is bound up in fear demands security and protection. When this is the case, we build self-defense mechanisms that keep us from living spontaneously in terms of the other. In Macmurray's words, "The more fear there is in us, the less alive we are. Fear accomplishes this destruction of life by turning us in upon ourselves and so isolating us from the world outside us."[81] Fear is part of the human condition; but the Father wants to set us free, so He comes to us time and again saying, "Fear not," "Fear not," "Do not be afraid."

To be sure, God doesn't promise that in this life we will be spared from suffering, loss, unhappiness or death. In fact, Jesus says it clearly:

> *I have said these things to you, that in me you may have peace. In the world you will have tribulation. But take heart;*
> *I have overcome the world.*
>
> John 16:33

Notice He is not saying that those things we fear will never happen to us. We live in a broken world, and therefore, we are subject to the consequences of sin (including human free will and demonic influence). There will come a day when Jesus will reign fully on earth, God's will shall be done perfectly, and all these things will pass away. But in the meantime, we will have trouble. We will experience pain, suffering, and death; but Jesus reassures us that we don't need to live in fear because He has overcome the world. It's not that we won't experience the things that we fear; but we don't have to be ruled by them. Even in adverse circumstances, we can have the assurance that God is with us and will see us through. There is no defeat in life, unless we allow circumstances to separate us from His love.[82] When we are assured of *Abba's* love for us, we can enjoy real freedom—the freedom where we don't have to look after our own interests, so we can truly live in other-centered, fullness of life.

Jesus' Fear-Free Life

Jesus shows us the clearest picture of this abundant life. As the fulfilled human in perfect relationship with the Father, He shows us what it's like to live in true freedom. Perhaps the best-known example of His other-centered life is seen in the Upper Room, as He is sharing the last Passover meal with His disciples:

> [Jesus] *rose from supper. He laid aside his outer garments, and taking a towel, tied it around his waist. Then he poured water into a basin and began to wash the disciples' feet and to wipe them with the towel that was wrapped around him.*
>
> John 13:4-5

What a great example to follow! Jesus was taking the posture of the most menial of servants, showing what it means to live with an other-centered orientation—not looking to our own interests but to the interests of others (Philippians 2:4).

Our problem, however, is that we often consider Jesus' actions and assume we are called to imitate Him by our own willpower. We attempt to condition ourselves to make the right choices and discipline ourselves to act rightly. We think if we just try harder, we might someday learn to live holy lives, as Jesus did. But I want to draw your attention to the preceding verse, which shows us Jesus' motivation and gives us a clue as to why He was able to serve so selflessly:

> *Jesus, knowing that the Father had given all things into his hands, and that he had come from God and was going back to God, rose from supper.*
>
> John 13:3-4

Jesus was secure in the Father's love. He knew where He had come from, and where He was going. Secure in *Abba's* love, He had nothing to prove, nothing to fear, and nothing to lose. (These characteristics of the spirit of sonship are explained in detail in *The Abba Factor*.) He didn't need the adulation of people to feel good about Himself. The love of

We think if we just try harder, we might someday learn to live holy lives.

His Father was all He needed. We see the same dynamic at work in Jesus' encounter with the devil in the wilderness: He was able to resist temptation because He was secure in His relationship with the Father.

Jesus was truly free, and therefore able to give freely of Himself.[83] In the loving relationship of the Triune God Jesus was free from fear—free from the need to look after His own interests, and thus free to love and be other-centered. This relationship empowered Jesus to endure suffering and lay down His life for humanity in service and obedience to His Father.[84]

Karl Barth says that God's high freedom in Jesus Christ is His freedom for love. God's freedom is manifested in that He can be in and for Himself, but also with and for us. He is the sovereign King; but He sacrifices Himself for our benefit. He is highly exalted; but He is completely humble. He is the almighty God who is full of mercy. He is Lord, but also servant. He is the judge, but takes on Himself the punishment for our sin. He is our eternal King, but also our brother in time.[85]

We are indeed called to imitate Jesus in His actions; but that is only possible when we experience true freedom—freedom from our fears and thus freedom from our need to self-protect, so we can give ourselves away, holding nothing back, loving our neighbor as ourselves.

The Solution: With-ness and For-ness

How, then, can we be free from fear? John tells us:

> *There is no fear in love, but perfect love casts out fear.*
> *For fear has to do with punishment,*
> *and whoever fears has not been perfected in love.*
>
> 1 John 4:18

The key to living a fear-free life is knowing God's perfect love—living in the awareness that God is both *with* us and *for* us. Both are important.

If we believe that God is *with* us, but we're not sure if He is *for* us, we may not want Him nearby.

If we believe God is *for* us, but we're not sure if He is *with* us, we remain fearful that He won't be around to help us in our need.

As we saw in earlier chapters, many of us have misconceptions about God that create a wedge between us and Him. These false notions of God cause us to question whether He is really *with* us or *for* us; but if we know the *Abba* of Jesus, we can know the perfect love of a good Father who wants the best for His children. Let's explore the biblical foundation for these two.

God Is With Us

In the majority of instances in Scripture where we see God telling His people not to fear, the command comes with the reassuring promise of His presence. Let's look at a few instances:

Fear not, for I am with you; be not dismayed, for I am your God;
I will strengthen you, I will help you,
I will uphold you with my righteous right hand.

Isaiah 41:10

It is the Lord who goes before you. He will be with you; he will not
leave you or forsake you. Do not fear or be dismayed.

Deuteronomy 31:8

God is our refuge and strength,
a very present help in trouble.
Therefore we will not fear though the earth gives way
though the mountains be moved into the heart of the sea.
The Lord of hosts is with us;
the God of Jacob is our fortress.

Psalm 46:1-2, 7

The Father doesn't call us to a stoic life in which we ignore the circumstances that would cause us to fear. On the contrary, He acknowledges that we don't have the capacity in ourselves to be free from fear, so He always reminds us of His commitment to be *with* us. There are many other verses that reaffirm God's commitment to be *with* us—not as momentary instances, but on a permanent basis:

My dwelling place shall be with them, and I will be their God,
and they shall be my people.

Ezekiel 37:27

Behold, the dwelling place of God is with man.
He will dwell with them, and they will be his people,
and God himself will be with them as their God.

Revelation 21:3

And they shall be my people, and I will be their God.

Jeremiah 32:38

And behold, I am with you always, to the end of the age.

Matthew 28:20

I will not leave you as orphans; I will come to you.

John 14:18

In His sovereignty, God has chosen to make His dwelling among humanity. He wants to be *with* us. In Chapter 3 we established that God creates as an overflow of the love shared between Father, Son, and Holy Spirit. God willingly creates a universe that He can fill with Himself and upon which He can pour His love. God didn't just create us to see if we would shape up and worship Him. On the contrary, He created us so He could share His being with us. He longs for us to live our lives *with* Him.

God Is For Us

Not only does God promise to be *with* us; but He also reveals Himself as the God who is *for* humanity. Over 70 times in the Old Testament God reveals Himself as our helper.[86] We see over and over how He comes to the rescue of His people, doing for them what they could never do on their own. Even when they faced impossible situations, they had the assurance of God's presence and help. The people of Israel knew that God was their defender, their deliverer, their provider, their helper, their healer, and their sustainer.

For I, the Lord your God, hold your right hand;
it is I who say to you, "Fear not,
I am the one who helps you."

Isaiah 41:13

Behold, God is my helper;
the Lord is the upholder of my life.

Psalm 54:4

In the same way, because we are His children through Jesus Christ, the Father comes to our aid time and again—not because we deserve it, but because He is loving and gracious. Scripture is clear to show that we didn't do anything to earn His love. His commitment to humanity was in place even before our hearts were turned toward Him. As Paul puts it:

But God shows his love for us in that while we were still sinners,
Christ died for us.

Romans 5:8

As great as the act of salvation is—Jesus dying on the cross for our sins—the incarnation is the greatest evidence that God is *for* humanity in every respect. By becoming human in the person of Jesus Christ, God committed Himself forever to the human cause. Karl Barth says:

In Jesus Christ there is no isolation of man from God or God from man. Rather, in [Jesus Christ] we encounter the history, the dialogue, in which God and man meet together and are together, the reality of the covenant mutually contracted, preserved, and fulfilled by them.[87]

Jesus and the Father enter into covenant on behalf of humanity, and God himself fulfills the covenant in Jesus. Whatever God wants to give humanity, He gives through Jesus. And whatever God wants to receive from humanity, Jesus himself fulfills on our behalf.[88]

God is not waiting for us to get our act together so He can bless us. No! His desire is to be *with* us, dwelling *in* us by His Spirit, calming our fears and persuading us of His love *for* us. He wants us to know His love and be convinced that He is *for* us, so we can be free from fear and experience fullness of life.

So great is God's commitment to be *with* and *for* humanity, that in the New Testament Jesus promises the coming of the Holy Spirit, calling Him *allos parakletos*—literally meaning "another one who is

Whatever God wants to give humanity, He gives through Jesus.

called alongside to help" (John 14:16).[89] The triune God comes, by the Holy Spirit, to those who will receive Him—to be with us, to heal us, to change us, to teach us, and to empower us for fullness of life. Paul tells Timothy:

> *For God gave us a spirit not of fear but of power*
> *and love and self-control.*
>
> 2 Timothy 1:7

Freedom from fear is not something God does to us; it's what He does by dwelling in us by the Holy Spirit. He has not given us a spirit of fear, but His own Spirit, which transforms us from the inside-out. With the indwelling Holy Spirit, we are no longer subject to the frailty of the human condition, but rather empowered to experience eternal life—the God-kind of life.

The Indwelling Holy Spirit

Since the Holy Spirit is the helper sent by the Father (as Jesus promised), it's good for us to take some time to explore some of the many things He does in our lives. Of course, any attempt to enumerate the manifold work of the Holy Spirit is sure to fall short. Among others, He instructs, regenerates, sanctifies, comforts, speaks, testifies, orders, reveals, creates, teaches, convicts, searches, strengthens, inspires and guides.[90] However, specific to the notion of freedom and how we grow into maturity toward full personhood and fullness of life, there are several aspects of His work that warrant elaboration.

Holy Spirit Mediates the Love and Presence of God

By the Holy Spirit, we can experience the indwelling presence of God—not as a detached counterpart, but as an all-embracing presence. We come to know God's love in an intimacy that exceeds the human notion of relationship. Notice Paul's prayer for the Ephesians:

He is not only with us and for us; but He is in us.

> *For this reason I bow my knees before the Father*
> *… that according to the riches of his glory he*

may grant you to be strengthened with power through his Spirit
in your inner being, so that Christ may dwell
in your hearts through faith—that you, being rooted
and grounded in love, may have strength to comprehend with all
the saints what is the breadth and length and height and depth,
and to know the love of Christ that surpasses knowledge,
that you may be filled with all the fullness of God.
Ephesians 3:14-19

The love of God is far greater than our minds can comprehend; but the Holy Spirit gives us revelation—spiritual insight—to experience the love of God. Through the Holy Spirit we never have to wonder if God is near. He is not only *with* us and *for* us; but He is *in* us. Could we ever doubt His presence or His commitment to be our helper?

Holy Spirit Gives Us Hope

The Spirit gives hope and meaning to our lives by communicating the presence of eternity and casting temporal human existence in eternal perspective. This *eschatological* hope is the source of the power to endure suffering *with* Christ.[91] The Holy Spirit sustains and helps us in the midst of suffering and weaknesses.[92] As mentioned earlier, this doesn't imply that we will never have to face any trials.[93] What it does mean is that the Holy Spirit gives us boldness in the face of opposition, the ability to love and forgive, and the freedom to "refuse honors, to submit to insults with goodwill, to despise himself and welcome disparagement; to bear all adversity and loss, and to desire no kind of prosperity in this world."[94] The Spirit gives us hope, and with it the power to live in freedom to respond to God's activity, even in the face of adversity.

Holy Spirit Forms Us

Our life in Christ, as children of God, is a process of transformation. When we accept what Jesus has done on our behalf, the Holy Spirit comes to dwell in us. We are born again.[95] Once we are born of the Spirit, He himself works in us to conform us to the image of Christ. Jack Hayford explains this process of "Spirit formation" with the analogy of hot air balloons that illustrate the difference between being "Spirit filled" and

"Spirit formed." He says that any balloon can be filled with air and float (as balloons do); but there are particular balloons (like the ones used in the Macy's Thanksgiving Day Parade) that, when filled with air, take on a particular form that the crowd can recognize. As born-again believers, we are to be both filled with the Spirit *and* formed by the Spirit into the likeness of Jesus, so that others can see Jesus in us and be attracted to Him. Spirit-fullness has as inward application: God living *in* us, while Spirit-formation has an outward application: God living *through* us.[96]

In the process of Spirit-formation, the Holy Spirit nullifies the power of sin and leads us from false believing into right believing. He guides, encourages and empowers us to endure suffering; and He sets us free to become grateful, hopeful persons who live—as Christ did—the loving, compassionate, forgiving, selfless, giving, healing, welcoming life of the Father.[97] By the Spirit, we not only come to know God, but we get to live in His presence "in such a way as constantly to be renewed into God's image."[98]

Holy Spirit Empowers Obedience

An outcome of Spirit-formation is a life of obedience in response to God's initiative. It's important for us to know that we don't become obedient by self-effort, but by the transforming work of the Holy Spirit. As Paul says:

> *Therefore, my beloved ... work out your own salvation with fear and trembling, for it is God who works in you, both to will and to work for his good pleasure.*
> Philippians 2:12-13

Note that the "working out of our own salvation" is explained through the work of the Holy Spirit. It's a partnership. As we allow Him, the Holy Spirit writes God's Law in our hearts.[99] He changes our want-tos, and then gives us the power to live accordingly. Therefore, the key to a life of freedom is a life of obedience; and the key to a life of obedience is summed up in Paul's imperative:

> *Walk by the Spirit, and you will not gratify the desires of the flesh.*
> Galatians 5:16

The Holy Spirit is the active agent of this transformation. When we are formed by the Holy Spirit and assured of the Father's love for us, we can be free from self-centeredness, guilt, fear of death, and outside pressures. "Freedom in Christ produces a healthy independence from peer pressure, people-pleasing, and the bondage of human respect."[100] With this freedom, we can concern ourselves with the character and desires of God. Knowing we are accepted, we can accept others; freed from ourselves, we can liberate others and share in their suffering.[101] These characteristics of other-centered freedom are summed up in the "fruit of the Spirit."

We can't work hard enough to produce the fruit by mere human effort.

The Fruit of the Spirit

According to Paul, the fruit of the Spirit is love, joy, peace, patience, kindness, goodness, faithfulness, gentleness, and self-control (Galatians 5:22-23). Peter speaks of us as partakers of the divine nature and lists faith, virtue, knowledge, self-control, steadfastness, godliness, brotherly affection and love (2 Peter 1:3-11). James describes these as "wisdom from above" and gives as examples purity, peace, gentleness, willingness to yield, mercy, impartiality and sincerity (Jas. 3:17-18). These are all manifestations of the Spirit at work in our lives. These are not behavioral lists, but rather a sampling of manifestations of God's life in and through His children.[102]

Given that God is a loving relationality, and God's desire is for humanity to become a reflection of Himself, it's no surprise that "love" is first in Paul's description of the fruit of the Spirit. Joy, hope, and peace are an overflow of God's way of being.[103] Longsuffering, kindness, goodness, faithfulness, gentleness and self-control are attitudes that foster healthy community life—the type of life that reflects God's way of being.[104] The fruit of the Spirit—the outflow of His work in our lives—is the key to relational wholeness.

Before we turn to that, let me reiterate that the fruit of the Spirit cannot be fabricated. We can't work hard enough to produce the fruit by mere human effort. This would not be the fruit of the Spirit, but the fruit of human willpower. We can, however, allow the fruit to ripen by itself, as we yield to the Holy Spirit, receiving through Him the love and presence of God, allowing Him to form us, to change our desires, and to empower us to live according to God's will.

Freedom and Relational Wholeness

In the last chapter we mentioned that the horizontal guidelines from the Ten Commandments are fulfilled when we are rightly related to God. As we have seen here, God's perfect love—mediated by the Holy Spirit— sets us free from fear, self-centeredness and self-protection, enabling us to live other-centered lives that reflect His nature. Said another way, when we know the love of the Father we are secure in His love, and thus, we are whole. When we are whole, we know we have nothing to fear, nothing to prove, nothing to hide, and nothing to lose. This sets us free to be other-centered, like the Father, Son, and Holy Spirit. This way of being fulfills the last six commandments (or "words"):

> *Honor your father and your mother, that your days may be long*
> *in the land that the Lord your God is giving you.*
> Exodus 20:12

When you know that in the Father you are totally loved, completely accepted, and perfectly secure, you don't look to your parents for what you can receive from them. Your love for them won't be conditioned by how perfect or imperfect they are, but you can look for ways to share the unconditional love of God to them and honor them.

> *You shall not murder.*
> Exodus 20:13

When you know that in the Father you are totally loved, completely accepted, and perfectly secure, you won't even contemplate the desire that someone's life be cut short for your benefit. Jesus said hatred is equivalent to murder. He is speaking of the attitude that says, "I wish you were dead!" We may think that our lives would be better if we could dispose of certain people; but as we let the unconditional love of God flow through us, we can see others the way God sees them. We are empowered to forgive and bless even our worst enemies. Therefore, when we are whole in Him, we shall not murder.

You shall not commit adultery.

Exodus 20:14

When you know that in the Father you are totally loved, completely accepted, and perfectly secure, you won't have a need to satisfy sexual urges in unwholesome ways. When there is brokenness and we feel that something is lacking in our lives, we may try to filling the void with passions of the flesh. But these only leave us wanting more. By contrast, when we are filled with the love of the Father, we won't feel the need to fill a void. We can find our fullness in Him. Therefore, when we are whole in Him, we shall not commit adultery.

You shall not steal.

Exodus 20:15

When you know that in the Father you are totally loved, completely accepted, and perfectly secure, you won't try to get what you need by taking it from others. You know that God is a good Father who will supply all your needs. This being the case, why would you steal?

You shall not bear false witness against your neighbor.

Exodus 20:16

When you know that in the Father you are totally loved, completely accepted, and perfectly secure, you won't look for ways to exalt yourself by putting others down. When we are insecure, we look for ways to feel better about ourselves. This can involve gossip, false accusations, or judgments. But if we are whole in God, we can celebrate each other's successes knowing that our worth is not diminished in the least, because it's determined by our Father—and our Father alone.

*You shall not covet your neighbor's house; you shall not covet your
neighbor's wife, or his male servant, or his female servant, or his
ox, or his donkey, or anything that is your neighbor's."*

Exodus 20:17

When you know that in the Father you are totally loved, completely accepted, and perfectly secure, you won't covet what others have. If we think our worth is determined by our achievements or material possessions, we will look for ways to get ahead, even if it means stepping on others as we climb the "ladder of success." When we think we need to self-protect, we may lie and cheat to get what we think we need. But when we know the love of God, we learn to be content with what we have. We can relax, secure in His love.

Conclusion

In this chapter we have said that true freedom is not the absence of problems, hindrances, or confinement. It's not the ability to do whatever we want; but on the contrary, the freedom from self-preservation; the freedom from the need to look after our own interests. It's the freedom to be other-centered; the freedom to respond to God without fear or hesitation. It's the freedom to choose life and live in holiness. The greatest obstacle to this life of freedom is fear, for it leads us to live on the defensive and look out for ourselves. But God reminds us that He is *with* us and *for* us, so we have nothing to fear.

For us to live in freedom, God has given us His Holy Spirit who mediates the love and presence of God, gives us hope, forms us into the likeness of Jesus, changes our desires, and empowers us to live according to the Father's perfect will. All this by the power of the Spirit. The fruit of the Spirit is the key to relational wholeness; and as such, the key to fullness of life.

- Because we are totally loved, totally accepted, secure in God's love—we are free to serve.
- Because we are totally loved, totally accepted, secure in His love—we are free to love others.
- Because we are totally loved, totally accepted, secure in His love—we are free to give of ourselves to others.
- Because we are totally loved, totally accepted, secure in His love—we are free to be holy, even as He is holy.

REFLECTION

Think (or ask the Holy Spirit to remind you) of a difficult or painful situation in your life where you questioned whether God was with you. Ask Him the following questions. With each one, be silent and allow Him to speak to you. He might answer you with a word, a picture, a vision, or a sense in your spirit. Agree with Him with whatever He shows you:

- *Abba*, where were You when this happened?
- *Abba*, how did You feel when this happened?
- *Abba*, what do You want to say to me about this situation?
- *Abba*, is there a lie that I have believed about You because of this situation?
- *Abba*, what do You want to give me in exchange for that pain?

PRAYER

Father, I thank You that You are always with me, and You are for me. Even in those times that I didn't feel Your presence, I acknowledge that You have been by my side. I thank You for sending Jesus to take all my pain, my weakness, and my fear, and to make me whole. I receive Your perfect love, which casts out all fear. Grant me to be strengthened with might through the Holy Spirit in my inner man, that Christ may dwell in my heart through faith; that I, being rooted and grounded in love, may be able to comprehend with all the saints what is the width and length and depth and height—to know the love of Christ which passes knowledge; that I may be filled with all Your fullness. In Jesus' name. Amen.

(see Ephesians 3:16-19)

Chiqui Wood

GROUP DISCUSSION

1. Contrast the notion of freedom *from* and freedom *to*. How is the idea of freedom in Christ different from the ideas of freedom held by those who don't know Christ?

2. Discuss why fear is the greatest inhibitor of other-centered action. Can you think of some examples of this?

3. How does knowing that God is *with* us and *for* us help us in living a life of holiness?

4. Which aspect of the work of the Holy Spirit in our lives strikes you the most? Why?

Nine

The Father's Gifts

If you, then, though you are evil, know how to give good gifts to your children, how much more will your Father in heaven give good gifts to those who ask him!

—Jesus

God will never ask of us anything that He doesn't first give us. He is a giving God. This is seen all throughout Scripture, but is best exemplified in one of his earliest revelations of Himself.

In Genesis 22 we find a shocking interaction between God and Abraham. After waiting patiently for the fulfillment of God's promise, Abraham and Sarah give birth to Isaac. And now, some years later, God asks Abraham to offer Isaac as a burnt offering. Wait! What? Many passages in the Old Testament make it clear that this practice is detestable to God.[105] But now God is asking Abraham to do the very thing He abhors. Why would God do that?

I have heard it said that God wanted to put Abraham to the test—to test his faith—as if He didn't know what Abraham was going to do. Another possibility is that God wanted Abraham to know where his own faith was. But I want to offer you a different possibility.

Think about this: Abraham had come out of Ur of the Chaldeans. He was a pagan, and in this culture it was a common practice to offer their sons to Molech—their god—as a way to demonstrate their allegiance to him. The mindset was that through this form of worship, they could get on the gods' "good side;" then the gods would be pleased with them and do favors for them.

In this interaction between God and Abraham, God was dealing with Abraham according to his context—in terms that Abraham could understand. It's as though God was saying, "Go ahead; that's your practice; that's how you think things work. Go ahead and do it. Offer me your son."

Our Father is a giving God. Abraham was doing something that was completely normal for him. It seems crazy to us because we live in a different world with different customs; but for him it was perfectly normal that a god would ask for that kind of sacrifice. So, Abraham goes along with the plan. He has no problem with it. In fact, we get a glimpse into Abraham's relationship with God. He knows there is something different about this God, because he tells Isaac, "My son, God will provide for Himself the lamb for a burnt offering."

Just as Abraham anticipated, when he is about to slay his son, the Angel of the Lord stops him and shows him a ram that was caught in a thicket. Abraham takes the ram and offers it as a burnt offering instead of his son.

> *So Abraham called the name of that place, "The Lord will provide."*
> Genesis 22:14[106]

The point of this story is this: God reveals Himself in a most unique way: "I am not like the other gods. I am not like the gods that you have served and that your people have served. I am not asking *you* to sacrifice for *my* benefit. I, the Lord, will provide my own offering." God reveals something of His nature. He's revealing Himself as a God who gives; as God, the provider. This is His nature. Our Father is a giving God. He doesn't withhold good things. He's not looking for what we can give to Him; but on the contrary, He delights in giving good things to us. Jesus said:

> *If you then, who are evil, know how to give good gifts to your children, how much more will your Father who is in heaven give good things to those who ask him!*
> Matthew 7:11

Abba is a giving Father. What does He give? This is what we address in this chapter.

God Gives of Himself

First, God gives of Himself. We need to understand that everything God gives is primarily a giving of Himself. In earlier chapters we established that God's way of being is infinite, overflowing, outgoing, self-giving love. Because God is love, God is self-giving. We see this in the act of creation, the act of redemption, and the process of restoration.

God Gives of Himself in Creation

In the act of creation, we see God giving of Himself. Recall the narrative of the creation of humanity:

> *Then God said, "Let us make man in our image, after our likeness.*
> *And let them have dominion over the fish of the sea and over the*
> *birds of the heavens and over the livestock and over all the earth*
> *and over every creeping thing that creeps on the earth."*
> *So God created man in his own image, in the image of God he*
> *created him; male and female he created them.*
> Genesis 1:26-27

God had created the planets, water, land and sky, and all types of animals. But when He creates humanity, He does something unique. From the Genesis 1 narrative all we know is that God created us; but in Genesis 2 we see a clearer picture that shows how God gives of Himself to give us life:

> *Then the Lord God formed the man of dust from the ground*
> *and breathed into his nostrils the breath of life,*
> *and the man became a living creature.*
> Genesis 2:7

Not only did God form each of us, but He has given us the spirit of life. John says both that God is a spirit (John 4:24), and that in Jesus was life (John 1:4; 11:25). As humans, we have life because God has given a deposit of Himself to us. With every breath we take we can be reminded that we have life only because *Abba* is a giving Father who gives of Himself.

Not only does God give us the breath of life, but He gives us gifts—unique personalities, traits, talents and abilities—as His seal of ownership.[107]

With every breath we take we can be reminded that we have life only because *Abba* is a giving Father who gives of Himself.

God created humanity as His partners in ruling over creation. The triune God—Father, Son and Holy Spirit—could do everything He wants to do by simply speaking a word; but He has chosen to involve you and me—even in our limitations—to fulfill His plan for the entire created universe. To this end, God has made a deposit of Himself in each one of us, and calls us to use those gifts to serve others as a reflection of His life in us, and as a testimony of His goodness.

God Gives of Himself in Redemption

As we saw earlier, God's original intent was for us to enjoy fullness of life in relationship and partnership with Him (Father, Son, and Holy Spirit). But when Adam and Eve ate of the Tree of the Knowledge of Good and Evil, they essentially chose to live a life independent of their Creator. This separation from God, which results in self-sufficiency and self-centeredness, brings spiritual death. God's desire for us didn't change, but we had no power in ourselves to restore the relationship and receive new life. We needed salvation, so God took the initiative to redeem us and bring us to life again.

In the act of redemption, we see God giving of Himself:

For God so loved the world, that he gave his only Son,
that whoever believes in him should not perish but have eternal life.
John 3:16

As my mentor, Wess Pinkham, likes to say, "When God gives a gift, He wraps it in a Person. He doesn't just send a message. He sends a Person." God loved the world so much that He gave His Son. God himself came to us in the form of Jesus—fully God, and fully man. God became one with us and gave us salvation. If God was after judicial satisfaction, a simple decree would have been enough; but He is after relationship, so everything He does, He does relationally. He doesn't just give salvation as a gift; but He himself becomes the gift. In the Person of Jesus Christ, we are saved.

God Gives of Himself in Restoration

Jesus' act of redemption initiates a process of restoration for each of us—and for all creation. In this process of restoration, we see God giving of Himself once again. On the last night Jesus spent with His disciples before going to the cross, He promised the coming of the Holy Spirit:

> *And I will ask the Father, and he will give you another Helper,*
> *to be with you forever, even the Spirit of truth, whom the world*
> *cannot receive, because it neither sees him nor knows him. You*
> *know him, for he dwells with you and will be in you. I will not*
> *leave you as orphans; I will come to you.*
>
> John 14:16-18

True to His promise, after Jesus was crucified but before He ascended to the Father's right side, Jesus met His disciples in Capernaum:

> *He breathed on them and said to them, "Receive the Holy Spirit."*
>
> John 20:22

At that point His disciples were born again—born of the Spirit into newness of life. Whenever we receive Jesus as our Lord and Savior, He breathes on us and we receive the Holy Spirit. God himself comes to dwell in us, to lead us and guide us into all truth, to teach us, and to give us everything we need to fulfill the Father's perfect will for our lives.

After Jesus breathed on His disciples, He told them to go to Jerusalem and wait. The Father was about to give even more. God has not called us to walk out this life by our own effort, but He himself gives us the power we need to participate in His mission and thus experience fullness of life. Jesus told His disciples:

> *And behold, I am sending the promise of my Father upon you.*
> *But stay in the city until you are clothed with power from on high.*
>
> Luke 24:49

This promise was fulfilled in Acts 2. When the Day of Pentecost had come, they were all in one accord, in an upper room in Jerusalem.

> *And suddenly there came from heaven a*
> *sound like a mighty rushing wind, and it*
> *filled the entire house where they were sitting.*
> *And divided tongues as of fire appeared to*

The Holy Spirit is active in the world today to fulfill the Father's mission.

them and rested on each one of them.
And they were all filled with the Holy Spirit and began to speak
in other tongues as the Spirit gave them utterance.

Acts 2:2-4

Jesus said they would be clothed with power from on high. What is this power, promised by the Father and proclaimed by Jesus? None other than God himself—God the Holy Spirit. This same promise is available to us today. We receive the Holy Spirit in overflow measure; and through the Holy Spirit we receive everything the Father has for us.[108] The Holy Spirit is active in the world today to fulfill the Father's mission of restoring all creation back to His original intent.

Some of the ways in which He works are described in 1 Corinthians 12 as "manifestation of the Spirit, given for the profit of all." Where there is need for discernment, the Holy Spirit manifests God's love, compassion and power through a word of wisdom, a word of knowledge, or discerning of spirits. Where there is need for edification, exhortation, comfort, or direction, the Holy Spirit manifests God's love, compassion and power through a prophecy, or a message in an unknown tongue along with the interpretation of the same. Where there is a need for specific things to be done, the Holy Spirit manifests God's love, compassion and power through a gift of faith, gifts of healings, or the working of miracles. All of these manifestations are supernatural. They transcend human capability, but are usually given by the Holy Spirit through human vessels who are willing to partner with Him in His mission of restoration.[109]

As we have seen, in the act of creation God gives of Himself. In the act of redemption God gives of Himself. And in the process of restoration God gives of Himself. *Abba* is a giving Father who gives of Himself. By His grace, He gives us everything we need including peace, joy, healing, wisdom, and provision.

Grace

Since everything God gives is an act of grace, before looking briefly at the Father's gifts, we must clarify what we mean by God's grace. The most common definition of grace is "God's unmerited favor." This means that whatever God gives us, He does willingly. We don't have to earn it.

In fact, we can't. The Father's goodness toward us stems from His way of being—which is love—and not by anything we have done (or could ever do) to deserve it. A few additional definitions will give us a greater understanding of God's grace.

In 2 Corinthians 12, Jesus himself defines grace in practical terms. Paul had been asking God about the "thorn in the flesh"[110]—something that kept causing him trouble wherever he went. Paul calls it a "messenger of Satan to buffet me." Clearly this was a source of discomfort, and something that Paul considered a hindrance to his life and mission. Jesus responds to Paul's plea saying:

> *My grace is sufficient for you, for my power*
> *is made perfect in weakness.*
>
> 2 Corinthians 12:9

Here Jesus defines grace in practical terms as "God's power at the point of our weakness, our need." Applied to salvation, God himself came to our rescue and did for us what we could not do for ourselves. This is grace. But the application is much broader than just salvation. God makes Himself available to us; so, whatever our weakness may be, His power is available to help us.

According to the *Exegetical Dictionary of the New Testament*, the Greek word *charis* (grace) was used in non-Christian writings to refer to free, uncoerced, cheerfully bestowed openness toward one another.[111] This was the understanding of the original setting in which the New Testament writers described God's way of being toward us. We have already seen that God freely gives of Himself, not because we are deserving but because it's His way of being. The love of the Father, Son, and Holy Spirit is such that God gives of Himself freely, uncoerced, and cheerfully. Our God is a compassionate God, who invites us to draw near and ask Him for what we need:

> *For we do not have a high priest who is unable to sympathize*
> *with our weaknesses, but one who in every respect has been*
> *tempted as we are, yet without sin. Let us then with confidence*
> *draw near to the throne of grace, that we may receive mercy and*
> *find grace to help in time of need.*
>
> Hebrews 4:15-16

What are some things we need? And how does God give them to us? We don't have space to cover every possibility, but exploring a few salient ones should convince us of God's willingness to give of Himself to meet our every need.

Peace

Peace is a fruit of the Holy Spirit—it's something He produces in us by His presence. In fact, when Jesus is speaking to His disciples, He promises a gift of peace:

> *These things I have spoken to you while I am still with you. But the Helper, the Holy Spirit, whom the Father will send in my name, he will teach you all things and bring to your remembrance all that I have said to you. Peace I leave with you; my peace I give to you. Not as the world gives do I give to you. Let not your hearts be troubled, neither let them be afraid.*
>
> John 14:25-27

Notice that Jesus declares that His peace is unlike the world's notion of peace. In the world, peace is the absence of problems. But Jesus knows that in this broken world we will have tribulation, and yet promises a different kind of peace. This is peace in the midst of the storm. It's the peace mediated by the presence of the Holy Spirit. He himself is our peace. When we are in His presence, our troubles come into perspective. This is why Paul says:

> *Do not be anxious about anything, but in everything by prayer and supplication with thanksgiving let your requests be made known to God. And the peace of God, which surpasses all understanding, will guard your hearts and your minds in Christ Jesus.*
>
> Philippians 4:6-7

The peace of God passes all human understanding because it's not circumstantial. When we are in His presence, we can have peace.

Joy

Joy is a byproduct of abiding in the Father's love.

Joy is a byproduct of abiding in the Father's love. It's a fruit of the Spirit that doesn't depend on circumstances. David says:

You make known to me the path of life;in your presence there is fullness of joy;at your right hand are pleasures forevermore.
Psalm 16:11

And Jesus proclaims:

As the Father has loved me, so have I loved you. Abide in my love.
If you keep my commandments, you will abide in my love,
just as I have kept my Father's commandments and abide in his love. These things I have spoken to you, that my joy may be in you, and that your joy may be full.
John 15:9-11

As with peace, we can be in the midst of trouble and still have joy. We can be in deep sorrow—even in grief—and still have joy. Joy is a quality of knowing that, in God, everything is well. It doesn't mean that we ignore our situation. It's not a matter of stoicism, but a gift of God's presence. The world may be crumbling around us, but we know that we are safe in the Father's arms. Whatever we may go through, when we abide in the Father's love, we can have His gift of joy.

Wisdom

We tend to think of wisdom as applied knowledge, gained from experience (and usually attained from bad experiences). If we live cautiously, we are generally considered to be "wise." But godly wisdom is far more than that. James tells us:

If any of you lacks wisdom, let him ask God, who gives generously to all without reproach, and it will be given him.
James 1:5

Wisdom is neither a thing nor an attribute of God. Wisdom is a person. Jesus is the wisdom of God. With our cultural definition we interpret that to mean that God will help us learn what we need to know in order to be successful in life, or perhaps to somehow understand the mysteries of living in a broken world. However, God is inviting us to ask Him for a different kind of wisdom.

The Hebrew understanding of wisdom is not just knowledge, but the ability to do God's will. Wisdom is practical. It's both knowledge of God's world and His Word, as well as the ability to do God's will in personal, daily life as well as in the life of the community. So, God tells us in James that with His wisdom, we not only have the knowledge of what to do, but He also gives us the ability, the power to do it. How? By giving of Himself.

Paul says that Christ is the power and wisdom of God (1 Corinthians 1:24). A few verses later he says that Jesus "became to us wisdom from God." Therefore, we see that wisdom is neither a thing nor an attribute of God. Wisdom is a person. Jesus is the wisdom of God. When we ask God for wisdom, we aren't asking Him for a thing, but for more of Himself.

God freely gives us, in himself, the wisdom we need so we can live into all He has purposed for us. Paul declares:

For we are his workmanship, created in Christ Jesus for good works, which God prepared beforehand, that we should walk in them.
Ephesians 2:10

We don't plan our own good works, but we seek to discover and then enter into the good works God has already planned for us. We need the guidance of the Holy Spirit, because He both reveals and leads us into God's plan for our lives.

In 1 Corinthians 2:9-16, Paul declares that our human reasoning can't comprehend the things that God has prepared for us who love Him; but that God has revealed them to us through His Spirit. (This is addressed in detail in *The Abba Formation*.) He goes on to say that we have the mind of Christ. This means that we possess the wisdom of God that has been incarnated in Christ as we are joined to Him as part of His Body by the Spirit. The Holy Spirit has been freely given to us so that we may freely know how to walk in the things that God has prepared for us. If we live by what we can comprehend with our natural mind, we will miss out on the greater plans that God has for us; but when we live a life of Spirit-fullness, we enter into a new dimension of living that far exceeds our expectations. This is where we find abundant life.

Healing

God also gives us healing. This is part of His mission of restoration. While we don't necessarily see God's will done perfectly on earth (i.e. not everyone is healed), the Bible is clear in demonstrating that healing is ordinarily God's will. This can be seen in three primary areas. First, God's name *YHWH Rapha*:

> *If you will diligently listen to the voice of the Lord your God,*
> *and do that which is right in his eyes, and give ear to his*
> *commandments and keep all his statutes, I will put none of the*
> *diseases on you that I put on the Egyptians,*
> *for I am the Lord, your healer.*
> Exodus 15:26

After the Israelites crossed the Red Sea, God revealed Himself as *YHWH Rapha*, meaning, "I am the Lord your healer," or "I am the Lord, who heals you." In this revelation, He clearly demonstrated His will regarding health and wholeness. Healing is not just something that God does, it is who He is. Healing is part of His nature.[112]

Second, healing is a benefit of the cross. In His death, Jesus took upon Himself all our infirmities:

> *But he was pierced for our transgressions;*
> *he was crushed for our iniquities;*
> *upon him was the chastisement that brought us peace,*
> *and with his wounds we are healed.*
> Isaiah 53:5

Matthew comments on this passage from Isaiah, noting that Jesus cast out evil spirits and healed all who were sick in order to fulfill what Isaiah had spoken:

> *That evening they brought to him many who were oppressed by*
> *demons, and he cast out the spirits with a word and healed all*
> *who were sick. This was to fulfill what was spoken by the prophet*
> *Isaiah: "He took our illnesses and bore our diseases."*
>
> Matthew 8:16-17

Isaiah looked forward to the benefits of the cross; Jesus lived them out during His earthly ministry. Peter, looking back at the cross, confirms that healing has already been provided:

> *He himself bore our sins in his body on the tree,*
> *that we might die to sin and live to righteousness.*
> *By his wounds you have been healed.*
>
> 1 Peter 2:24

Third, and most importantly, we know that healing is the Father's will because, as we have established, Jesus reveals the character of the Father. A look at Jesus' miracles and His attitude toward sickness reveals *Abba's* heart concerning healing. Since Jesus went about healing all who were oppressed of the devil, we know that the Father's character is hostile against sickness.[113]

Many of us have had experiences where we have sought God for healing (of ourselves or a loved one), and have not received the expected result. When faced with this mystery, we must remember that God's will is not done perfectly on earth. When dealing with sickness, we are confronting sin, demonic beings, and a host of complex psychological, physical and spiritual factors.[114] But let us not get confused about the character of our Father. God is always good. He always wants the best for us. There are always things beyond our understanding; but we can trust His love and remember that He is our healer, and He's working on our behalf.

Provision

Provision is another gift from God that is rooted in who He is. As we saw in the introduction to this chapter, in Genesis 22 one of God's earliest self-revelations is that He is YHWH Jireh, "the Lord will provide." This is demonstrated in Jesus' ministry where we see that Jesus met a variety of needs. In some instances He provided food for the hungry (Mark 6:34-44; 8:1-9, Matt. 14:13-21; 15:32-39; Luke 9:12-17; John 6:5-6). He helped His disciples meet their financial obligations (Matt. 17:24-27). We even see Jesus providing something as seemingly trivial as wine for a wedding (John 2:1-11). In the parable of the Prodigal Son, Jesus shows us the clearest picture of *Abba* and He is portrayed as a generous Father who shares all His resources with His children. He is not stingy!

On the Sermon on the Mount, Jesus makes a statement about *Abba's* care for us. He tells us that we need not worry, for the Father doesn't want us to suffer lack:

> *Therefore I tell you, do not be anxious about your life, what you will eat or what you will drink, nor about your body, what you will put on. Is not life more than food, and the body more than clothing? Look at the birds of the air: they neither sow nor reap nor gather into barns, and yet your heavenly Father feeds them. Are you not of more value than they? And which of you by being anxious can add a single hour to his span of life?*
> *And why are you anxious about clothing? Consider the lilies of the field, how they grow: they neither toil nor spin, yet I tell you, even Solomon in all his glory was not arrayed like one of these. But if God so clothes the grass of the field, which today is alive and tomorrow is thrown into the oven, will he not much more clothe you,*
> *O you of little faith?*
> *Therefore do not be anxious, saying, 'What shall we eat?' or 'What shall we drink?' or 'What shall we wear?' For the Gentiles seek after all these things, and your heavenly Father knows that you need them all. But seek first the kingdom of God and his righteousness, and all these things will be added to you. Therefore do not be anxious about tomorrow, for tomorrow will be anxious for itself. Sufficient for the day is its own trouble.*
> Matthew 6:25-34

God is a generous provider. As His children, we can rest assured that we will have what we need to have when we need to have it. However, in light of *Abba's* generosity, Jesus warns us against getting

We will have what we need to have when we need to have it.

151

Prosperity: "Having all we need to do God's will, with enough left over to be generous on every occasion."

carried away with materialistic, consumerist notions of provision. He promises to meet our needs, not necessarily our wants.

Take care, and be on your guard against all covetousness, for one's life does not consist in the abundance of his possessions.
Luke 12:15

In our Western context, we think that wealth and poverty are the greatest determinants of well-being; so, when we talk about provision, the first thing that comes to mind is material provision. But God is concerned with far more than that. His desire is for us to have everything we need to do His will—be it material resources, wisdom, revelation knowledge, healthy relationships, opportunities, abilities, or the like. Dallas Willard says it this way: "Under the rule of God, the rich and the poor have no necessary advantage over each other with regard to well-being or well-doing in this life or the next."[115] God, by His grace, gives us what we need to fulfill our purpose and enjoy fullness of life. In Paul's words:

God is able to make all grace abound to you, so that having all sufficiency in all things at all times, you may abound in every good work ... He who supplies seed to the sower and bread for food will supply and multiply your seed for sowing and increase the harvest of your righteousness. You will be enriched in every way to be generous in every way, which through us will produce thanksgiving to God.
2 Corinthians 9:8, 10-11

This verse gives us a good definition of prosperity: "Having all we need to do God's will, with enough left over to be generous on every occasion." Notice that by His grace, God provides much more than material resources. Remember that we defined grace as God's strength (or power) at the point of our need. We can expand that definition to say that grace is God's provision at the point of our need. He himself comes to our aid, no matter what our weakness may be. In this verse Paul reiterates Jesus' promise that the Father will supply what we need when we need it.

God, our provider, gives us much more than material possessions.

He gives us things of a richer quality—those intangible things that money can't buy. As we have seen, by His grace God gives us joy, peace , wisdom, and health. By His grace, God also gives us insight, knowledge and understanding:

> *I still have many things to say to you, but you cannot bear them now.*
> *When the Spirit of truth comes, he will guide you into all the truth,*
> *for he will not speak on his own authority, but whatever he hears*
> *he will speak, and he will declare to you the things that are to come.*
> *He will glorify me, for he will take what is mine and declare it to*
> *you. All that the Father has is mine; therefore I said that he will*
> *take what is mine and declare it to you*
>
> John 16:12-15

God is not a cosmic vending machine, obligated to give us whatever we want; but neither is He reluctant to resource us with what we need. Jesus compares the Father's generosity with our own and lets us know, in no uncertain terms, that *Abba* is far more generous than we realize:

> *Ask, and it will be given to you; seek, and you will find; knock,*
> *and it will be opened to you. For everyone who asks receives, and the*
> *one who seeks finds, and to the one who knocks it will be opened.*
> *Or which one of you, if his son asks him for bread, will give him*
> *a stone? Or if he asks for a fish, will give him a serpent? If you then,*
> *who are evil, know how to give good gifts to your children, how*
> *much more will your Father who is in heaven give good things to*
> *those who ask him!*
>
> Matthew 7:7-11

Moreover, Jesus tells us that we can be bold in asking *Abba* for what we desire:

> *If you abide in me, and my words abide in you,*
> *ask whatever you wish, and it will be done for you.*
>
> John 15:7

Notice, however, that this is conditional. There is a relational quality that opens the door for us to confidently ask the generous Father what we desire. When we abide in Him, and let His words abide in us, then our desires will be calibrated to His desires. As we saw in the last chapter, when we allow Holy Spirit to work in our lives, He changes our want-to's, and then gives us the power to live accordingly. In the same way, the posture of intimacy that Jesus describes—abiding in Him—calibrates our heart with what the Father wants for us. Then we can ask boldly, knowing we will receive whatever we ask.

Of course, there is a sense in which the Father gives us gifts, neither because we need them, nor because we want them, but simply because He wants to show us how much He loves us. We call those, " *Abba* hugs." *Abba* hugs can be as simple as a little flower hiding under a tree in the Grand Canyon hiking trail, so delicate and beautiful that when I find it, I can't help but smile. An *Abba* hug can be a perfect sunset at the end of a busy day. An *Abba* hug can be a stranger we meet on our vacation who just happens to be the local expert and gives us directions to the most beautiful site in town. An *Abba* hug can be any number of things that remind us that He loves and cares for us. If we look for them, we'll find that *Abba* hugs are far more frequent than we realize.

Conclusion

In this chapter we have said that *Abba* is a giving Father. He reveals Himself as our provider. However, what He provides is not separated from who He is. In the act of creation, God gives of Himself. In the act of redemption God gives of Himself. And in the process of restoration God gives of Himself. The Holy Spirit is active in the world to fulfill the Father's mission of restoration. He gives gifts that manifest God's love, compassion and power to restore creation back to God's original intent. This is all a work of grace—God's strength at the point of our need. By God's grace, we can have peace. By God's grace, we can have joy. By God's grace, we have wisdom both to know and to do His perfect will. By God's grace, we can receive healing. And by God's grace, we can receive everything we need to fulfill our purpose and enjoy fullness of life. How does God distribute His gifts in the earth? He does so through human cooperation. As we shall see in the next chapter, the Father invites us to partner with Him in His mission.

REFLECTION

On the Sermon on the Mount, Jesus says that we need not worry about what we shall eat, what we shall drink, or what we shall wear, for our Father knows that we need them. The implication is that He will take care of our needs.

- What are some things that you worry about? What do you think Jesus would say to you about those things?
- Are there any things that cause you anxiety? What do you think Jesus would say to you about those things?
- Do you have any specific needs in your life? What do you think Jesus would say to you about those things?

PRAYER

Father, we thank You that You are our provider; that You are a generous Father, and that You take care of our every need. Thank You for giving of Yourself on our behalf. You didn't have to, but Your love is so great that You continue to give, even though we don't deserve it. Forgive me for the times I have taken You for granted; for the times I have failed to thank You for Your goodness toward me. For those times when I have not received what I expected as an answer to my prayers, I choose to trust You and ask You to fill me with Your joy and peace. I surrender that situation to You. I declare that You are a good Father, and I choose to rest in You. In Jesus' name. Amen.

GROUP DISCUSSION

1. How does understanding God's grace as His strength at the point of our need help you in approaching God confidently in prayer?

2. Can you think of some hindrances that keep us from receiving the many gifts that the Father gives? What can we do to overcome them?

3. Make a "gratitude list" of as many things as you can identify that God has freely given you. You may want to include some "*Abba* hugs." Share the list with your group, and explain how making such a list can be helpful in deepening your relationship with God.

Ten

The Father's Call

Come to me, all who labor and are heavy laden, and I will give
you rest. Take my yoke upon you, and learn from me, for I am
gentle and lowly in heart, and you will find rest for your souls.
For my yoke is easy, and my burden is light.

—Jesus

Throughout this book we have focused on who God is. Since what we believe about God determines what we believe about everything else, we established a foundation that has implications on every area of our lives. Our starting point is realizing that God—Father, Son, and Holy Spirit—has existed eternally in a relationship of infinite, other-centered, overflowing, self-giving love. With that understanding we looked at the Father's creation, His will, His mission, His gifts, and His expectations and desires for us, showing that they all flow out of His way of being, which is love. Because God is overflowing, infinite love, He created a universe, and beings with whom He could share His love. Because God is overflowing, infinite love, His desire is to restore everything that has been broken by sin. Because God is overflowing, infinite love, He took the initiative to save us—to make us whole, restored in relationship with Himself. Because God is overflowing, infinite love, He gives us everything we need to experience fullness of life—life as God has it. Father, Son and Holy Spirit created us both for relationship and for partnership. This is abundant life!

Now we must ask what our part is. How should we live in light of who God is, what He has done for us, and what He freely gives us? How do we respond to the Father's invitation to fullness of life? In earlier chapters we said that, given that God created us in His image, we experience fullness of life when we cultivate whole and healthy relationships with Him and with one another. We conclude our journey together by considering

God's will for your life is that you be *with* Him. that we experience abundant, fulfilling lives when we respond to His call and participate in His mission of restoration.

Called to Be with Him

Pastors say the most frequent question their parishioners ask of them is "How can I know God's will for my life?" I can't give you a conclusive answer; but I can tell you this: The Father's will is that you be with Him. More important than anything that we do, the priority is being with Him. God created us for relationship, first and foremost. We see a glimpse of this in the record of Jesus calling His twelve disciples:

> And he [Jesus] *went up on the mountain and called to him*
> *those whom he desired, and they came to him. And he*
> *appointed twelve (whom he also named apostles) so that they*
> *might be with him and he might send them out to preach.*
> Mark 3:13-14

Jesus was calling them, and He would prepare them to preach and do miracles in His name; but this wasn't the priority. The priority was that they would be *with* Him. The same can be said for you. God's will for your life is that you be *with* Him. And out of this relationship He will prepare you, He will connect you with people, He will empower you, and He will show you the steps to take. But the priority is being with Him. Jesus makes this clear:

> On that day many will say to me, "Lord, Lord, did we not prophesy
> in your name, and cast out demons in your name,
> and do many mighty works in your name?"
> And then will I declare to them,
> "I never knew you; depart from me,
> you workers of lawlessness."
> Matthew 7:22-23

This may sound harsh; but it brings to light that to God, the priority is relationship. Above anything else, He wants to know us and to be known by us. He wants to have conversation with us. He longs for us to open our hearts to Him, to receive Him, to trust Him, to share with Him our thoughts, our feelings, our concerns, our joys and sorrows, our victories and defeats. I love the Psalms because in them

If we are to follow Jesus' example, let it be in this: that His life was all about His *Abba*.

we see that God can handle our honesty. We don't have to pretend that we've got it all together. Instead, we can come to Him with questions, with doubt, even with anger. He is not after our perfection, but our heart. *Abba* beckons us, time and again, to come to Him; and Jesus reminds us that abiding in Him is the key to fruitfulness:

> *Abide in me, and I in you. As the branch cannot bear fruit by itself, unless it abides in the vine, neither can you, unless you abide in me. I am the vine; you are the branches. Whoever abides in me and I in him, he it is that bears much fruit, for apart from me you can do nothing.*
> John 15:4-5

> *As the Father has loved me, so have I loved you. Abide in my love.*
> John 15:9

When we look at Jesus, we see what being fully human is all about. He was fully God and fully man; but everything He did on earth, He did as a human. He ministered in relationship with the Father and by the power of the Holy Spirit, to show us what fullness of humanity looks like—a life in perfect relationship with *Abba*. If we are to follow Jesus' example, let it be in this: that His life was all about His *Abba*.

How did Jesus have the power to overcome temptation? By His relationship with His *Abba*. Before He ever did anything, and before the devil tempted Him, Jesus had received His Father's affirmation:

> *And when Jesus was baptized, immediately he went up from the water, and behold, the heavens were opened to him, and he saw the Spirit of God descending like a dove and coming to rest on him; and behold, a voice from heaven said, "This is my beloved Son, with whom I am well pleased."*
> Matthew 3:16-17

Then the devil tempted Jesus three times with conditional statements: "If You are the Son of God ..." (Matthew 4:3-6) and "... if You will fall down and worship me" (Matthew 4:9). Each time Jesus responded by quoting Scripture:

> *He answered, "It is written, 'Man shall not live by bread alone, but by every word that comes from the mouth of God.'"*
>
> Matthew 4:4

> *"Again it is written, 'You shall not put the Lord your God to the test.'"*
>
> Matthew 4:7

> *"Be gone, Satan! For it is written, 'You shall worship the Lord your God and him only shall you serve.'"*
>
> Matthew 4:10

The temptation of the devil was clearly pointed, not at Jesus' calling or mission, but toward His identity as the Son of God—toward the relationship of love enjoyed by the Triune God. The devil's aim was not to get Jesus to break the Law (a judicial transgression), but to get Him to question His relationship with the Father. Jesus responded by quoting Scripture; but notably, the power to overcome was not that He "spoke the Word," but that in quoting Scripture, He was demonstrating His priority was the relationship which had just been lovingly affirmed by the Father.[116]

It is the same for us. Our power to overcome temptation is determined, not by our will-power or even how well we know Scripture, but by our relationship with *Abba*. When our identity is securely rooted in His love, we can face whatever comes our way without hesitation.

How did Jesus live in freedom to serve? His identity was rooted in His relationship with *Abba*. As we saw earlier, Jesus knew the Father had put all things under his power, and that He had come from God and was returning to God. He had nothing to hide, nothing to prove, nothing to fear, and nothing to lose. He was free because of His relationship with His Father. It's the same for us. Our freedom is rooted in the Father's love for us. (This is the freedom of the sons of God. *The Abba Formation* describes the work of the Holy Spirit to transform us from the inside-out.)

Our freedom is rooted in the Father's love for us.

How did Jesus know where to go, what to do, or what to say? He spent time with *Abba*. Jesus was consumed with the love of the Father. His life purpose was to do the work of the Father. Jesus himself said:

> *When you have lifted up the Son of Man, then you will know that*
> *I am he, and that I do nothing on my own authority, but speak just*
> *as the Father taught me. And he who sent me is with me. He has not*
> *left me alone, for I always do the things that are pleasing to him.*
> John 8:28-29

Jesus spent time with the Father, hearing His voice and receiving instructions for carrying out His mission. All through His ministry we see that He took time to pray. He didn't do anything without first talking with *Abba*:

> *Immediately [Jesus] made the disciples get into the boat and go*
> *before him to the other side, while he dismissed the crowds. And*
> *after he had dismissed the crowds, he went up on the mountain*
> *by himself to pray. When evening came, he was there alone.*
> Matthew 14:22-23

> *In these days he went out to the mountain to pray, and all night*
> *he continued in prayer to God. And when day came, he called his*
> *disciples and chose from them twelve, whom he named apostles.*
> Luke 6:12-13

> *And rising very early in the morning, while it was still dark, he*
> *departed and went out to a desolate place, and there he prayed.*
> Mark 1:35

> *And they went to a place called*
> *Gethsemane. And he said to his*
> *disciples, "Sit here while I pray."*
> Mark 14:32

> *But he would withdraw to desolate*
> *places and pray.*
> Luke 5:16

Just as Jesus cultivated His relationship with *Abba* by spending time with Him, it's important for us to cultivate our relationship with the Father.

Just as Jesus cultivated His relationship with *Abba* by spending time with Him, it's important for us to cultivate our relationship with the Father. It's of utmost importance for us to learn to hear His voice—the voice of a Father who is continually speaking. The words He speaks to us are spirit and life (John 6:63). His words are our primary spiritual nourishment. As Jesus said:

Man shall not live by bread alone,
but by every word that comes from the mouth of God.
Matthew 4:4

Can you imagine having a relationship with someone with whom you never communicate? That would be ridiculous! It's the same with God. If we want to cultivate a relationship with Him, we must engage in dialogue with Him. This is where spiritual disciplines such as prayer, Bible study, worship, fasting, or fellowship, come into play.[117]

Let's be clear. The purpose of spiritual disciplines is not to prove what great Christians we are; neither to develop our will-power, nor to earn good standing with God. We don't do things *for* God in order to be loved or accepted. We don't do things *for* God in order to receive His benefits. As we have seen, The Father loves us because we are His. It's not that God loves us because we are valuable; rather, we are valuable because God loves us! And since He loves us, He blesses us because it's His nature to give good gifts. We didn't do anything to deserve His love, and there's nothing we can do to keep Him from loving us; but it's up to us whether we receive His love. As Tillich suggests, faith is the courage to accept our acceptance.[118] We can choose to receive God's love and live in relationship with Him, or reject it and try to make it on our own.

The purpose of spiritual disciplines, rather, is to create opportunities for encounters with *Abba*. We practice spiritual disciplines to talk to God and hear Him speak to us. It's in those encounters that we receive His love, His acceptance, His grace, His gifts, and His power. In the Father's presence we are healed and find freedom from the wounds of our past. Hearing the Father speak, we come to know ourselves as He knows us. Hearing the Father's voice, the lies of the enemy are exposed and replaced by the affirming words of a loving Father. (The progression from an orphan spirit to a spirit of sonship is detailed in *The Abba Factor.*) By hearing the Father's voice, He creates realities in us that did not exist before or calls out purpose that we have yet to discover. In the Father's presence, we are made whole. Spending time with God we mature as His children and become agents of reconciliation. Cultivating encounters with the Father, the fruit of the Spirit is produced in our lives. In those encounters our hearts are filled with so much love that we can't keep it to ourselves.

We are called, first and foremost, to *be* with God. Out of that relationship, however, we are also called into mission. We are called to partner with Him. As we shall see, in this partnership is fullness of life.

Called to Participate in His Mission

Jesus' life was rooted in His relationship with *Abba*. Because of their intimate relationship, Jesus was all about the Father's mission. He exemplifies for us fullness of life as a life of partnership with God. He says:

> *My food is to do the will of him who sent me*
> *and to accomplish his work.*
>
> John 4:34

> *I glorified you (Abba) on earth, having accomplished the work*
> *that you gave me to do.*
>
> John 17:4

His ministry was to do the will and work of the Father, and so it is with us. Because we are His, the Father calls us to partnership. He invites us to participate in His mission. He created us for relationship and partnership, and has sovereignly determined that He will not execute His will on earth, except through human cooperation. As partners with God, we can pray for His will to be done. As partners with God, we become vessels of His grace, distributing His gifts to heal the brokenness of the world.

When God formed you, He did so according to a particular design, for a particular purpose. He has great plans for your life. We must clarify again, as we did with spiritual disciplines, that participation in mission is not a condition for acceptance. We

He will not execute His will on earth, except through human cooperation.

163

don't do things *for* God in order to be loved or accepted. Instead, we do things *with* God because we are His children. We work *with* God, because we know the joy of partnership. We minister to others because we know the fulfillment of seeing God work *in* and *through* us. We *do*, not because we are coerced, but because we accept the grand invitation of the Father. We participate in His mission because His love compels us, and because we know that in doing so, we experience abundant life. As we said earlier, God's will for your life is that you be with Him. In this relationship He will prepare you, connect you with people, and show you the steps to take.

How do we participate in the Father's mission? Any attempt to define what is "acceptable participation" would bring us back to a place of religiosity—as though partnership was about mere obedience with no regard for relationship. Instead, we say that it can take many forms, including (but not limited to) compassion, solidarity, intercession, power encounters, evangelism, social justice, fellowship, celebration, or forgiveness. It can take place in the every-dayness of life. Living with God is what gives life meaning. Consequently, anything we do can be done in partnership with Him. Any opportunity we take to let the love of God flow in and through us is a form of participation—whether loving our spouse and children, or being single and devoting our life to Him; whether serving our employer as an act of devotion to Him, or serving one another with the gifts and talents we have graciously received from God.[119]

Of course, to fully understand what a life of partnership with *Abba* looks like, we look again at Jesus' life. As we noted earlier, His was a life consumed with the Father's mission. His ministry was to do the will and work of the Father (John 4:34; 9:4; 17:4). However, He did not meet the needs of every person He encountered. He did only what He saw the Father doing, and He did it in the power of the Holy Spirit:

> *God anointed Jesus of Nazareth with the Holy Spirit and with power. He went about doing good and healing all who were oppressed by the devil, for God was with him.*
>
> Acts 10:38

In like manner, *Abba* doesn't call us to meet the needs of every person we encounter, but simply to be attentive to His prompting in order to let

Him work through us. The work of the ministry to which *Abba* calls us is always initiated, empowered and guided by the Holy Spirit. It's the overflow of God's presence, God's love and acceptance that forms us and moves us to share it with others. We are called to live in overflow fullness. Filled with the Holy Spirit, His love overflows through us. This is abundant life!

Called to a Lifestyle of Spirit-Fullness

Remember that God's way of being is infinite, overflowing, other-centered love. By "overflowing" we mean that the Father, Son, and Holy Spirit can't keep their love to themselves. This infinite love demands expression, and His desire for us is that we also experience the life of overflow where we can't help but give out of the love we receive from Him.

There is a great word in Scripture to denote this overflow: the Greek word *pleroma*, which is usually translated as *fullness*. This word indicates "a full measure, copiousness, plenitude, that which has been completed." It strongly emphasizes fullness and completion, the idea of being filled to overflowing.[120] *Pleroma* is used in several places in the New Testament, as in this prayer of Paul for the Ephesians:

> *For this reason I bow my knees before the Father, from whom every family in heaven and on earth is named, that according to the riches of his glory he may grant you to be strengthened with power through his Spirit in your inner being, so that Christ may dwell in your hearts through faith—that you, being rooted and grounded in love, may have strength to comprehend with all the saints what is the breadth and length and height and depth, and to know the love of Christ that surpasses knowledge, that you may be filled with all the fullness of God.*
> Ephesians 3:14-19

Paul's desire is that we be filled—overflowing—with all the fullness—overflow—of God. This is more than our minds can comprehend. God doesn't just want us to be filled unto ourselves, but to receive so much from Him that we can't keep it to ourselves. When we allow Him to fill us, participation in His mission is inevitable. Jesus said it this way during the Feast of Tabernacles:

> On the last day of the feast, the great day, Jesus stood up and cried out, "If anyone thirsts, let him come to me and drink. Whoever believes in me, as the Scripture has said, 'Out of his heart will flow rivers of living water.'" Now this he said about the Spirit, whom those who believed in him were to receive, for as yet the Spirit had not been given, because Jesus was not yet glorified.
>
> John 7:37-39

According to Paul, living in the fullness of the Spirit is the key to our life in Christ:

> But I say, walk by the Spirit, and you will not gratify the desires of the flesh ... If we live by the Spirit, let us also keep in step with the Spirit.
>
> Galatians 5:16, 25

Paul doesn't see being filled with the Spirit as an optional extra. He says, in no uncertain terms:

> Be filled with the Spirit.
>
> Ephesians 5:18

In the original language, this command is in the present, passive, imperative tense. Because it is present tense, it implies a continual action. Because it is passive, it means that we are the recipients of the action. Finally, because it is imperative, Paul indicates that this is not an option. In the Greek language, this simple imperative is the most forceful way to tell someone to do something. Paul expects those addressed to do exactly as he has ordered.[121]

Accept. Believe. Ask the Father. Receive by faith. And finally, cultivate a life of fullness.

Being filled with the Spirit is best seen as a person-centered experience in which God encounters His people in the person of His Spirit. God initiates it, and our part is simply to receive. How do we enter this life of Spirit-fullness?

First, accept the Father's free gift of salvation through Jesus:

And this is eternal life, that they know you, the only true God, and
Jesus Christ whom you have sent.

John 17:3

And it shall come to pass that everyone who calls upon
the name of the Lord shall be saved.

Acts 2:21

Then believe the promise of the Holy Spirit is for you:

Peter said to them, "Repent and be baptized every one of you in the
name of Jesus Christ for the forgiveness of your sins, and you will
receive the gift of the Holy Spirit. For the promise is for you and for
your children and for all who are far off, everyone whom the Lord
our God calls to himself."

Acts 2:38-39

Ask the Father:

And I tell you, ask, and it will be given to you; seek,
and you will find; knock, and it will be opened to you.
For everyone who asks receives, and the one who seeks finds, and
to the one who knocks it will be opened. What father among you,
if his son asks for a fish, will instead of a fish give him a serpent; or
if he asks for an egg, will give him a scorpion? If you then, who are
evil, know how to give good gifts to your children, how much more
will the heavenly Father give the Holy Spirit to those who ask him!"

Luke 11:9-13

Receive by faith:

And this is the confidence that we have toward him, that if we ask
anything according to his will he hears us. And if we know that he
hears us in whatever we ask, we know that we have the requests
that we have asked of him.

1 John 5:14-15

And finally, cultivate a life of fullness, following Paul's example and instruction:

Be filled with the Spirit, addressing one another in psalms
and hymns and spiritual songs, singing and making melody
to the Lord with your heart.
                                                      Ephesians 5:18-19

Let the word of Christ dwell in you richly, teaching and
admonishing one another in all wisdom, singing psalms and hymns
and spiritual songs, with thankfulness in your hearts to God.
                                                      Colossians 3:16

What am I to do? I will pray with my spirit,
but I will pray with my mind also; I will sing praise with my
spirit, but I will sing with my mind also.
                                                      1 Corinthians 14:15

When we are filled with the Spirit, we come to know God's love to such a degree that it moves us to love others. When we are filled with the Spirit, His holiness fills us and flows out of us. When we are filled with the Spirit, participating in mission is not a chore, but a natural outworking of His life in us. When we are filled with the Holy Spirit, we receive from God everything we need to fulfill His plan for our lives. When we are filled with the Spirit, we experience eternal life in the fullest sense of the word.

Conclusion

In this final chapter we have said that *Abba's* greatest desire is that we be with Him. He made us for relationship and partnership; but the relationship is primary. Abiding with *Abba* is the key to fruitfulness. Abiding with *Abba* gives us power to overcome temptation. Abiding with *Abba* sets us free for a life of service—a life of purpose—as we participate with Him in His mission of restoration. Just as Jesus cultivated His relationship with *Abba* by spending time with Him, so we practice spiritual disciplines as opportunities for encounter. We practice spiritual disciplines to talk to God and hear Him speak to us. Hearing the Father's voice is the catalyst to our freedom and transformation.

We are also called into mission—not as a condition for acceptance, but as a response to His love. The work of the ministry to which *Abba* calls us is always initiated, empowered and guided by the Holy Spirit. It's the overflow of God's presence, God's love and acceptance that forms us and moves us to share it with others.

Finally, we are called to live in overflow fullness. Living in the fullness of the Spirit is the key to our life in Christ. Living a life of fullness is as simple as (1) accepting the Father's free gift of salvation through Jesus; (2) believing the promise of the Holy Spirit is for you; (3) asking the Father and receiving by faith; and finally, (4) cultivating a life of Spirit-fullness by following Paul's example and instruction. When we allow Him to fill us, participation in His mission is inevitable, and abundant life becomes a reality.

The Father is calling you to know Him—intimately and deeply. He wants to save you, strengthen you, and give you abundant life. He calls you into a life of being with Him and partnering with Him in His mission. Will you accept His call?

REFLECTION

Consider what it means that the Father desires to be with you. More than anything else, He wants your presence. To finish this journey, I want to share with you an adaptation of reflection from Brennan Manning:

- Do you ever reflect upon the fact that God—Father, Son, and Holy Spirit—feels proud of you? Proud that you accepted the faith which He offered you? Proud that you chose Jesus for a friend and Lord? Proud of you that you haven't given up? Proud that you believe in Him enough to try again and again? Proud that you trust that He can help you?
- Do you ever think that *Abba* appreciates you for wanting Him, for refusing those things that distract you from Him?
- Do you ever think of God rejoicing over you for your heart to know Him intimately, and share that knowing with others?

- Do you think that *Abba's* heart swells over you for your pausing to smile, comfort, give to one of His children who have such great need to see a smile, to feel a touch?[122]

Have you been trying to *do* things *for* Him? Could it be that you subconsciously feel like you need to do things to deserve His love? Is there any area in your life that may make you hesitant to spend time with *Abba*? The Father is longing for you to come into His presence and is waiting for you with open arms. Run to His embrace!

PRAYER

Abba, I belong to You. Thank You for forming me and calling me to Yourself. Thank You for engrafting me into Your mission. Thank You for allowing me to partner with You; what a privilege that is! I give You my life, my heart, my hands and feet. Open my eyes, that I may see You more clearly. Open my ears, that I can hear Your voice. Open my heart, and enlarge my capacity to receive everything You have for me. Fill me with Your Spirit, that You may overflow through me. Make me a vessel of Your goodness to the world. May others see Jesus in me. Teach me how to live fully as Your son/daughter. In Jesus' name, Amen.

GROUP DISCUSSION

1. Since the purpose of spiritual disciplines is to create opportunities for encounters with *Abba*, discuss the spiritual disciplines that you practice.

2. Which new spiritual disciplines can you use as means to welcome His presence and cultivate a life of spiritual overflow?

3. Do you have a sense that the Father is calling you into partnership with Him? What might that look like given the way He has formed you and prepared you thus far?

Epilogue

What you have seen and heard in these pages is intended to paint a different picture of the Father, perhaps very different from the stern, austere God that many of us grew up knowing as Almighty God. Yes, He is nothing short of almighty, but He is more. Do you see His eyes of love, His overflowing passion toward you? Do you hear the patience in His voice, the gentle beckoning of a father who cannot be hurried by time, because He is larger than time itself? Thus, He is projecting no pressure upon you—no impulsive tapping of the foot that says, "What could be taking you so long? Hurry up child!"

And there is more. Have you seen in these pages that the Father's thoughts toward you are so good, and His vision so clear as to what He has purposed for you, that there is no room in His heart for the petty ideas that you won't arrive there? He is already speaking to you as one who is sitting at His right hand. But do you hear His laughter; His joy and delight in you? Do you not yet see Him dancing about you and singing raucous songs of fun and anticipation over you?

If that picture, of the God that calls for feasts and parties, isn't an easy one for you yet, I invite you to continue your *Abba* journey by reading *The Abba Factor* and *The Abba Formation*.

In *The Abba Factor*, you will see yourself through the Father's eyes, and will understand the progression from an orphan spirit to the spirit of sonship.

In *The Abba Formation*, you will learn to partner with the Holy Spirit, who searches the Father's heart, discloses His purposes to you through spiritual words, and restores you to a child-likeness that sees the universe as the Father's playground for the sons and daughters He's redeemed for Himself.

My prayer for you is that the Father's voice grows more and more clear in your own spiritual ear, and resonates to the core of your being, *"You are my beloved son/daughter, in whom I am well pleased."*

Endnotes

[1]Henri J. M. Nouwen, *A Cry for Mercy* (Garden City, NY: Doubleday & Co., 1981), 23.

[2]Ray S. Anderson, *The Soul of Ministry* (Louisville: Westminster John Knox Press, 1997), 32, 83.

[3]Brennan Manning, *The Ragamuffin Gospel: Embracing the Unconditional Love of God* (Sisters, OR: Multnomah Books, 1990), 14.

[4]Details can be found in my Doctor of Ministry Project: Ana Wood, "Relational Discipleship: The Formation of Persons in Relationship as the Foundation for Discipleship" (D.Min. proj., The King's University, 2014).

[5]Craig Haworth, "Different Views of Salvation" (Online Discussion in Spiritual and Personal Formation seminar, Kalona, Iowa, February 21, 2017), Shiloh University, Kalona, IA.

[6]Manning, *The Ragamuffin Gospel,* 75.

[7]Joachim Jeremias, *The Central Message of the New Testament* (London: SCM Press, 1965), 28-29.

[8]Jeremias, *The Central Message of the New Testament,* 9-21.

[9]Dallas Willard, *The Divine Conspiracy: Rediscovering Our Hidden Life in God* (San Francisco: HarperCollins, 1997), 391.

[10]Jeremias, *The Central Message of the New Testament,* 9-21.

[11]J.B. Torrance gives a caution against anthropomorphizing the notion of the word "Father:" "For us the word 'father' is a human class concept, which we predicate of creaturely male parents. How then can a word which is a human class concept be used to denote God who is not a member of that class? … If the human word 'father' is to be used of God, there must be a shift in meaning to denote God the Creator, who is the only true Father, after whom all earthly fatherhood is named (Eph 3:15). In the order of being, God's fatherhood is prior to ours, as the creator is prior to the creature. … We can only [compare and contrast God's fatherhood with ours theologically] by the content put into that word by Jesus Christ, as we reflect upon the life of Jesus, the words of Jesus, the sufferings of Jesus. We allow the Spirit, in interpreting Christ to us, to evacuate the word of all biological, male, patriarchal, sexist content, to fill it with divine content, that we may more truly pray, *"Abba, Father."* … the name [Father] is not merely an arbitrary signifier, like Susan or Fred! It has semantic content, as has the name of Jesus. It is the name through which God discloses

himself personally to us to draw us into intimate communion with himself in worship and prayer, not just to convey information about himself." James B. Torrance, *Worship, Community and the Triune God of Grace* (Downers Grove: IVP Academic, 1996), 123-5.

[12]A.W. Tozer, *The Knowledge of the Holy: The Attributes of God: Their Meaning in the Christian Life* (New York: Harper Collins, 1961), 2.

[13]Francis A. Schaeffer, *The God Who Is There* (Downers Grove: Inter-Varsity Press, 1968), 151-2.

[14]For a deeper look at the implication of knowing God the Father, see Chris Waters and Wess Pinkham. *Finding Closure to the Pains from the Past* (Lookout Mountain, TN: Journeys to the Heart, Inc., 2006), 18.

[15]For example, the Jewish people thought they had a corner on God, but when Jesus came on the scene He had to show them a whole different reality of who God is.

[16]In my first book, *Lessons Learned in the Battle,* I share the lessons I learned during my late husband's 5-year battle with Cancer. While I don't share definitive answers, the lessons are helpful in our struggle to find explanation and lean into the mystery of the trials of life. Chiqui Polo-Wood, *Lessons Learned in the Battle: How to Live in Victory, No Matter What* (Bedford, TX: Burkhart Books, 2015).

[17]Brennan Manning's comments on Flannery O'Connor's story, The Turkey, serve to illustrate how we project on to God our own attitudes and feelings as an unconscious defense of our sense of inadequacy or guilt. Brennan Manning, *A Stranger to Self-Hatred: A Glimpse of Jesus* (Denville, NJ: Dimension Books, 1982), 10.

[18]I owe the foundation of this section to Martin Folsom and Wesley M. Pinkham, *Relational Theology: A Primer* [CD-ROM] (Lookout Mountain, TN: Journeys to the Heart, 2002), 73, 113. Also Martin Folsom, "Relational Theology" (Lecture presented in the Relational Theology D.Min. seminar, Van Nuys, California, October 17-19, 2013) The King's University, Van Nuys, CA. For additional details on the Roman and Greek influences in Western thought and culture, see John Macmurray, *Freedom in the Modern World: Broadcast Talks on Modern Problems* (London: Faber & Faber Limited, 1934), 70-9.

[19]I don't have room to address this in detail in this book; but this is perhaps one of the reasons why so many in the Roman Catholic Church look to Mary as the mediator between them and God. After all, who would dare to approach the angry God? But Mary is human; she understands our condition, so we find it easier to

appeal to her. And since she is the mother of Jesus, she can intercede confidently on our behalf.

[20]Raymond Angelo Belliotti, *Roman Philosophy and the Good Life* (Plymouth, UK: Lexington Books, 2009).

[21]Waters and Pinkham. *Finding Closure to the Pains from the Past,* 32.

[22]A Greek philosopher named Heraclitus first used the term Logos around 600 B.C. to designate the divine reason or plan which coordinates a changing universe. In John, "the Word" denotes the essential Word of God, Jesus Christ, the personal wisdom and power in union with God, his minister in creation and government of the universe, the cause of all the world's life both physical and ethical, which for the procurement of man's salvation put on human nature in the person of Jesus the Messiah, the second person in the Godhead, and shone forth conspicuously from His words and deeds. "Lexicon: Strong's G3056 - *logos*," *Blue Letter Bible* (November 16, 2011), https://www.blueletterbible.org/lang/lexicon/lexicon. cfm?Strongs=G3056&t=ESV.

[23]"Genesis 1:26-27," *Blue Letter Bible* (November 16, 2011), https://www. blueletterbible.org/niv/gen/1/1/t_conc_1026.

[24]My mentor, Marty Folsom, and others, choose to use the pronoun "Godself" instead of "himself" to help us think differently in this regard. I prefer "Godself" (after all, it seems appropriate to use a unique pronoun for a God who is "wholly other") and considered using it in this manuscript. However, since "Godself" is not widely used in our language, for the sake of simplicity I will use "himself" but beg your understanding that by doing so I'm not ascribing specifically male characteristics to God.

[25]Chris Waters and Wess Pinkham explain that "Our Heavenly Father as "Relationship" resolves the gender problem that culture and language project onto His Being. He has both been described with male and female qualities. Attributing gender to our Heavenly Father has often resulted in the devaluation of women. As the Bible puts it: "There is neither Jew nor Greek, bond or free, male or female." Relationship is unity, interconnection (bonding) and fruitfulness. Waters and Pinkham. *Finding Closure to the Pains from the Past,* 24-25.

[26]Other scriptures where we see glimpses of the Trinity: John 3:34-35; John 15:26; John 16:14-15; Romans 8:3-4; Romans 14:17; 1 Corinthians 12:5-7; and 2 Corinthians 13:14. Scriptures that talk of the mutual indwelling of Father, Son and Holy Spirit: John 14:10, 11, 20; John

15:26; John 16:27, 32; John 17:11, 20, 22, 23, 26. Scriptures that talk of equality, love and shared mission of Father, Son and Holy Spirit: John 14:7, 9-11, 13, 16, 21, 23-24, 26, 31; John 15:7, 9-10, 15-16, 23-24, 26; John 16: 3, 5, 7, 13-14, 16, 23, 27-28; John 17:1-12, 18, 22-24.

[27] Clark H. Pinnock, *Flame of Love: A Theology of the Holy Spirit* (Downers Grove: IVP Academic, 1996), 35.

[28] Alistair I. McFadyen, *The Call to Personhood: A Christian Theory of the Individual in Social Relationships* (Cambridge: Cambridge University Press, 1990), 27.

[29] Colin E. Gunton, T*he Promise of Trinitarian Theology, 2nd ed.* (New York: T&T Clark Ltd., 1997), 12.

[30] Folsom and Pinkham, Relational Theology, 612.

[31] Thomas F. Torrance, *The Ground and Grammar of Theology* (Charlottesville: University Press of Virginia, 1980).

[32] Colin Gunton, *The One, the Three and the Many: God, Creation and the Culture of Modernity* (Cambridge: Cambridge University Press, 1998), 164.

[33] The dance metaphor has limited merit as an interpretive move as opposed to an etymological explanation. Nevertheless, the metaphor is helpful in creating an understandable picture of the fullness of life enjoyed through the relationship of the Father, Son, and Holy Spirit. See Thomas F. Torrance, *The Christian Doctrine of God: One Being, Three Persons* (Edinburgh: T & T Clark, 1996): 169-70.

[34] Karl Barth states that "In His life as Father, Son, and Holy Spirit He would in truth be no lonesome, no egotistical God even without man, yes, even without the whole created universe." Karl Barth, *The Humanity of God*, trans. John Newton Thomas and Thomas Wieser (London: Collins Clear-type Press, 1961), 50.

[35] Stanley Grenz explains: "Precisely because creation is God's loving act, it is free, voluntary, and non-necessary. At the same time, precisely because God is love, the act of creation naturally flows out of the inner life of the Triune One. Because God is the Trinitarian community of love, God need not create the world to actualize his character. Yet because God is love his creation of the world is fully in keeping with his character. Stanley Grenz, Theology for the Community of God (Grand Rapids: Eerdmans, 1994), 98-101.

[36] "Genesis 1:31," *Blue Letter Bible* (November 16, 2011), https://www.blueletterbible.org/niv/gen/1/1/t_conc_1031.

[37] In Genesis 2:7 we see that man was formed from the dust of the earth.

Everything else was made (Hebrew: 'asah), which means simply to do, work, make or produce. But when referring to the creation of man, the language is different. We read that man was formed (Hebrew: yatsar), which has the connotation of being formed, framed with a purpose, like a potter who forms the clay into a vessel for a particular purpose. "Genesis 2:7," *Blue Letter Bible* (November 16, 2011), https://www.blueletterbible.org/niv/gen/2/1/t_conc_2007.

[38]I'm assuming that most of my readers have been raised in the United States, or another Western country with similar values. If you were raised in a different culture, this may not be as significant to you; but it may give you some context for understanding how Westerners think, and why we need to emphasize this point.

[39]L. Robert Kohls had a doctoral degree in cultural history from New York University. He spent most of his career in the field of cross-culturalism as director of training for the U.S. Information Agency and the Meridian International Center in Washington. As Executive Director of The Washington International Center, in 1984 he wrote a monograph called "The Values Americans Live By." In this document he describes the 13 core values common to most Americans. L. Robert Kohls, "The Values Americans Live By," Claremont McKenna College, (January 10, 2017), http://www1.cmc.edu/pages/faculty/alee/extra/American_values.html

[40]Stoicism is one of the major Greek philosophical schools that influenced the intellectual and political leaders of the later Roman republic and early empire. Belliotti, *Roman Philosophy and the Good Life.*

[41]J. B. Torrance, *Worship, Community and the Triune God of Grace,* 37, 39.

[42]Folsom and Pinkham, *Relational Theology,* 520-22.

[43]John Macmurray, *Persons in Relation* (Atlantic Highlands, NJ: Humanities Press, 1979), 211.

[44]In Thomas J. Oord's, *The Uncontrolling Love of God,* he discusses seven models of God's providence: God is the omnicause; God empowers and overpowers, God is voluntarily self-limited, God is essentially kenotic, God sustains as impersonal force, God is initial creator and current observer, and God's ways are not our ways. Thomas J. Oord, *The Uncontrolling Love of God: An Open and Relational Account of Providence* (Downers Grove: IVP Academic, 2015).

[45]Manning, *The Ragamuffin Gospel,* 75.

[46]The Hebrews felt that what God commits; He permits. They did not distinguish between first and second cause. We must make a

distinction between what God permits (permissive will) and what God commits (directive will) concerning evil.

[47]In my first book, *Lessons Learned in the Battle,* I elaborate on the idea that the enemy steals, kills and destroys; but that's not his goal. These are just the tools that he uses for a greater purpose: to separate us from the love of God. However, even when the enemy has his way in bringing destruction in our lives, if we don't let that separate us from God's love, we have the victory. Polo-Wood, *Lessons Learned in the Battle,* 37-39.

[48]George Eldon Ladd presents the idea that the Kingdom of God is "now but not yet." Jesus inaugurated His kingdom—the rule of God on the earth—but it is not fully actualized yet. George Eldon Ladd, The Gospel of the Kingdom: Scriptural Studies in the Kingdom of God (Grand Rapids: Eerdmans, 1997).

[49]Roger T. Forster and V. Paul Marston, *God's Strategy in Human History* (Wheaton: Tyndale House Publishers, Inc., 1974), 34.

[50]Grenz, *Theology for the Community of God,* 108.

[51]Lillian B. Yeomans, *Healing Treasury: Four Classic Books on Healing, Complete in One Volume* (Tulsa, OK: Harrison House, 2003), 184.

[52]"John 3:17," *Blue Letter Bible* (May 29, 2017), https://www.blueletterbible.org/niv/jhn/3/17/t_conc_1000017.

[53]"Isaiah 49:6," Blue Letter Bible (May 29, 2017), https://www.blueletterbible.org/niv/isa/49/6/s_728006.

[54]The Greek word translated should and perish here is *apollymi,* which his Second Aorist, Middle, Subjunctive. The aorist tense is characterized by its emphasis on punctiliar action; that is, the concept of the verb is considered without regard for past, present, or future time. There is no direct or clear English equivalent for this tense, though it is generally rendered as a simple past tense in most translations. The Middle voice indicates the subject performing an action upon himself or for his own benefit. The Subjunctive mood indicates that the action described may or may not occur, depending upon circumstances. "John 3:16," *Blue Letter Bible* (May 28, 2017), https://www.blueletterbible.org/niv/jhn/3/16/t_conc_1000016

[55]The Greek word translated as have is *echō,* which is Present, Active, Subjunctive. The present tense represents a simple statement of fact or reality viewed as occurring in actual time. In most cases this corresponds directly with the English present tense. The Active voice represents the subject as the doer or performer of the action. The

Subjunctive mood indicates that the action described may or may not occur, depending upon circumstances. "John 3:16," *Blue Letter Bible* (December 15, 2011), https://www.blueletterbible.org/niv/jhn/3/16/t_conc_1000016.

[56]"John 3:16," *Blue Letter Bible* (December 15, 2011), https://www.blueletterbible.org/niv/jhn/3/16/t_conc_1000016.

[57]"John 10:10," *Blue Letter Bible* (December 17, 2011), https://www.blueletterbible.org/niv/jhn/10/10/t_conc_1007010.

[58]Barth, *The Humanity of God*, 73.

[59]This legal view is bolstered by Paul's use of very legal language in writing to a Roman audience in his letter to the Roman believers.

[60]Waters and Pinkham. *Finding Closure to the Pains from the Past*, 8.

[61]"Sin is primarily religious and secondarily ethical. Man is God's creature and his primary responsibility is toward God. The root of sin is found in his refusal to acknowledge in grateful dependence the gifts and the goodness of God (Rom. 1:21), which are now imparted in Christ. Darkness is the assertion of independence rather than God-dependence." George Eldon Ladd, *The Gospel of the Kingdom: Popular Expositions on the Kingdom of God* (Grand Rapids: Eerdmans, 1983), 31.

[62]These three aspects of holiness are derived from Grenz, *Theology for the Community of God*, 93-4.

[63]Waters and Pinkham. *Finding Closure to the Pains from the Past*, 27.

[64]Lexicon: *Strong's* G5046—*teleios*, "Blue Letter Bible" (November 9, 2011), https://www.blueletterbible.org/lang/lexicon /lexicon.cfm?Strongs=G5046&t=NIV

[65]James B. Torrance, *Worship, Community and the Triune God of Grace*, 52-3.

[66]The Hebrew word that is translated as commandments is dabar, which refers to speech, utterance, or words. "Commandments," *Blue Letter Bible* (December 15, 2011), https://www.blueletterbible.org/lang/lexicon/lexicon.cfm?Strongs=H1697&t=ESV.

[67]"Shall," *Merriam-Webster Dictionary Online*, (December 15, 2011), https://www.merriam-webster.com/dictionary/shall.

[68]Another example is Matthew 7:21-23 where people prophesy, cast out demons, and perform miracles and yet Jesus will say to them, "I never knew you." There was no relationship.

[68]This is seen most clearly in 1 Thessalonians 5:23—May God himself, the God of peace, sanctify you through and through. May your whole spirit, soul and body be kept blameless at the coming of our Lord Jesus Christ. Though this is an important subject, it is beyond

the scope of this study. Other authors have addressed the topic in greater detail.

[70]Rowan Williams, "Archbishop's address to the Synod of Bishops in Rome, Wednesday 10th October 2012" Dr. Rowan Williams, 104th Archbishop of Canterbury, (Published 2012), Accessed July 14, 2017, http://rowanwilliams.archbishopofcanterbury.org/articles/php/2645/archbishops-address-to-the-synod-of-bishops-in-rome.

[71]In the previous chapter we said that one of the ways we can understand God's holiness is in the way He relates to His creatures. We said that Father, Son, and Holy Spirit exist in a perfect relationship of love. As such, God is relationally whole; and from this wholeness, everything God does is other-centered. This other-centeredness is the essence of relational wholeness, which is the essence of holiness. Another way of saying this is, "holiness is wholeness in relationships." The Father would say, "if you want to be holy, cultivate whole relationships."

[72]Adapted from Jack W. Hayford, *Pastors of Promise: Pointing to Character and Hope as the Keys to Fruitful Shepherding* (Ventura: Regal Books, 1997), 198-199.

[73]This is one of many examples that show the Father's desire for all nations to know Him—Jew, Samaritan and Gentile alike.

[74]"Lexicon: *Strong's G4697 – splagchnizomai, Blue Letter Bible* (October 2, 2017), https://www.blueletterbible.org/lang/lexicon/lexicon.cfm?Strongs=G4697&t=ESV

[75]I must credit Kerry Wood for this phrase, which has been key to my understanding of holiness as relational wholeness.

[76]Matthew 5:43-48—"You have heard that it was said, 'Love your neighbor and hate your enemy.' But I tell you: Love your enemies and pray for those who persecute you, that you may be sons of your Father in heaven. He causes his sun to rise on the evil and the good, and sends rain on the righteous and the unrighteous. If you love those who love you, what reward will you get? Are not even the tax collectors doing that? And if you greet only your brothers, what are you doing more than others? Do not even pagans do that? Be perfect, therefore, as your heavenly Father is perfect."

[77]Macmurray, *Freedom in the Modern World*, 54-55.

[78]For additional help with addictions or other areas of bondage you may want to explore ministries like Cleansing Stream, or Nothing Hidden Ministries. Two excellent books that deal with freedom are Neil T. Anderson, *The Bondage Breaker* (Eugene, OR: Harvest House, 2006) and Henry Cloud and John Townsend, *Boundaries:*

When to Say Yes, How to Say No To Take Control of Your Life (Grand Rapids: Zondervan, 2017).

[79]N.T. Wright, *Following Jesus: Biblical Reflections on Discipleship* (Grand Rapids: Eerdmans, 1995), 66-7.

[80]Ibid.

[81]Macmurray, *Freedom in the Modern World*, 54-55.

[82]In my book, *Lessons Learned in the Battle*, I discuss the perspective that the enemy's goal is not to steal, kill or destroy. These are the tools that He uses for the purpose of separating us from the love of Christ. When we face adversity, if we don't let the circumstances separate us from His love, we always win. Polo-Wood, *Lessons Learned in the Battle*, 37-39.

[83]Karl Barth describes God's freedom as reflected in Jesus' life: "God's deity is thus no prison in which He can exist only in and for Himself. It is rather His freedom to be in and for Himself but also with and for us, to assert but also to sacrifice Himself, to be wholly exalted but also completely humble, not only almighty but also almighty mercy, not only Lord but also servant, not only judge but also Himself the judged, not only man's eternal king but also his brother in time. And all that without in the slightest forfeiting His deity! All that, rather, in the highest proof and proclamation of His deity." Barth, *The Humanity of God*, 49.

[84]Anderson, *The Soul of Ministry*, 31-2.

[85]Barth, *The Humanity of God*, 48-49.

[86]Seventy-five times in the Older Testament God is declared as helper: "Thou art the helper of the fatherless" (Ps. 10:14); "Hear, O LORD … be thou my helper" (Ps. 30:10); "Behold, God is mine helper" (Ps. 54:4); "For he shall deliver the needy when he crieth; the poor also, and him that hath no helper" (Ps. 72:12); "Unless the Lord had given me help …" (Ps. 94: 17); "You will increase my greatness, and comfort me on every side" (Heb. 13:6); "… so that we may boldly say, 'The Lord is my helper, and I will not fear what man will do to me'" (Ps. 71:21); "You have been my helper … teach me yours ways, O Lord." (Ps. 27:9). Kerry V. Wood, "Participating in the Ministry of Christ: The Contribution of Trinitarian Theology to an Understanding of the Nature of Pastoral Leadership" (D.Min. proj., The King's University, 2012), 110.

[87]Barth, *The Humanity of God*, 46-47.

[88]Barth elaborates on this theme saying, "Jesus Christ is in His one Person, as true God, man's loyal partner, and as true man, God's. He is the

Lord humbled for communion with man and likewise the Servant exalted to communion with God. He is the Word spoken from the loftiest, most luminous transcendence and likewise the Word heard in the deepest, darkest immanence. He is both, without their being confused but also without their being divided; He is wholly the one and wholly the other. Thus in this oneness Jesus Christ is the Mediator, the Reconciler, between God and man. Thus He comes forward to man on behalf of God calling for and awakening faith, love and hope, and to God on behalf of man, representing man, making satisfaction and interceding. Thus He attests and guarantees to man God's free grace and at the same time attests and guarantees to God man's free gratitude. Thus He establishes in His Person the justice of God's vis-à-vis man and also the justice of man before God. Thus He is in His Person the covenant in its fullness, the Kingdom of heaven which is at hand, in which God speaks and man hears, God gives and man receives, God commands and man obeys, God's glory shines in the heights and thence into the depths, and peace on earth comes to pass among men in whom He is well pleased. Moreover, exactly in this way Jesus Christ, as this Mediator and Reconciler between God and man, is also the Revealer of them both." Ibid.

[89] This implies that Jesus himself is our helper, and that Holy Spirit is a helper just like Him. The implication is that the triune God—Father, Son, and Holy Spirit—is the helper of humanity.

[90] Merrill F. Unger, *Unger's Bible Dictionary* (Chicago: Moody Press, 1979), 496; L. Berkhof, *Teología Sistemática,* translated by Felipe Delgado Cortés, (Grand Rapids, Eerdmans, 1979), 112; and Pinnock, Flame of Love, 115.

[91] Eschatology is the part of Theology that deals with the end-times. It has to do with looking toward the future state of the earth under the reign of Christ.

[92] Gordon D. Fee, *GOD's Empowering Presence: The Holy Spirit in the Letters of Paul* (Peabody: Hendrickson, 1994), 497.

[93] A false religion and idealism claims that life in Christ is a safeguard against the things that one fears. By contrast, true religion says that no matter what happens, there is nothing to fear. Macmurray explains it this way: "False religion and false idealism [say,] in effect: 'Shut your eyes to things you are afraid of; pretend that everything is for the best in the best of all possible worlds; and there are ways and means of getting the divine powers on your side, so that you will

be protected from the things you are afraid of. They may happen to other people, but God will see to it that they don't happen to you.' On the contrary, true religion says 'Look the facts you are afraid of in the face; see them in all their brutality and ugliness; and you will find, not that they are unreal, but that they are not to be feared." John Macmurray, *Freedom in the Modern World*, 59.

[94]Thomas à Kempis, *The Imitation of Christ* (London: Penguin Books, 1952), 87. Also Pinnock, Flame of Love, 116; and Graham H. Twelftree, People of the Spirit: Exploring Luke's View of the Church (Grand Rapids: Baker Academic, 2009), 107.

[95]Christianity is not about "following Jesus;" but about being born again – born of the Spirit. We are new creatures in Christ. If "following Jesus" was enough, then the people of Israel had everything they needed to experience eternal life. But when Jesus came, He came proclaiming among the Jews the need for them to be born again. In John 3 we find the story of Jesus speaking with Nicodemus – a ruler in the synagogue; a Pharisee. Nicodemus was a devout adherent of the Law of Moses; and yet Jesus says to him, "Most assuredly I say unto you, unless one is born again, he cannot see the kingdom of God" (John 3:3). He further clarifies it saying, "Unless one is born of water and the Spirit, he cannot enter the kingdom of God" (John 3:5).

[96]Jack W. Hayford, *Spirit-Formation* (Sermon Presented at the Autumn Leadership Conference, Van Nuys, California, 2000), The Church On The Way, Van Nuys, CA.; quoted in Wesley M. Pinkham, Identity Formation: The Journey toward Personhood (Lookout Mountain: Journeys to the Heart, Inc., 2003), 16.

[97]Wesley M. Pinkham and Chris Waters. Creative Conflict Management. Lookout Mountain: Journeys to the Heart, Inc., 2001), 292; and C. Baxter Kruger, The Great Dance: The Christian Vision Revisited (Vancouver: Regent College Publishing, 2000), 108. Also Pinnock, Flame of Love, 106, 178 and Jürgen Moltmann, The Spirit of Life: A Universal Affirmation (Minneapolis: Fortress, 1992), 278.

[98]Fee, *GOD's Empowering Presence*, 319.

[99]That God's laws would be written in our hearts speaks of the Father's desire for us to experience life in its truest sense, as expressed in Deuteronomy 5:29: "Oh, that they had such a heart in them that they would fear Me and always keep all My commandments, that it might be well with them and with their children forever!" See also Ezekiel 36:24-28 and Jeremiah 31:31-34 where God shows how holiness and

obedience to His Law are His own work in the heart of His people, by His Spirit.

[100]Brennan Manning, T*he Ragamuffin Gospel,* 151.

[101]Moltmann, *The Spirit of Life,* 99, 202; and Twelftree, People of the Spirit, 208-9.

[102]Jon Huntzinger, "Characteristics of the Holy Spirit" (Lectures presented in Biblical Resources for Ministry D.Min. seminar, Van Nuys, California, June 12, 2012), The King's University, Van Nuys, CA.

[103]Dallas Willard says of God's joy that "We should, to begin with, think that God leads a very interesting life, and that he is full of joy. Undoubtedly, he is the most joyous being in the universe. The abundance of his love and generosity is inseparable from his infinite joy. All of the good and beautiful things from which we occasionally drink tiny droplets of soul-exhilarating joy, God continuously experiences in all their breadth and depth and richness." Willard, *The Divine Conspiracy,* 62.

[104]For more elaboration on the fruit of the Spirit, how it was manifested in the life of Jesus and reflected in the Church, see Pinnock, *Flame of Love,* 37, 39, 117 and Twelftree, People of the Spirit, 108ff.

[105]Burning their sons in the fire as a sign of worship was common among the pagan people (see 2 Kings 17:31; 2 Kings 23:10; Leviticus 20; Jeremiah 32:35). Yet God says, "You shall not worship the Lord your God in that way, for every abominable thing that the Lord hates they have done for their gods, for they even burn their sons and their daughters in the fire to their gods" (Deuteronomy 12:31). He says "[the sons of Judah] have built the high places of Topheth, which is in the Valley of the Son of Hinnom, to burn their sons and their daughters in the fire, which I did not command, nor did it come into my mind" (Jeremiah 7:31). These people of Judah, "have built the high places of Baal to burn their sons in the fire as burnt offerings to Baal, which I did not command or decree, nor did it come into my mind" (Jeremiah 19:5).

[106]The Hebrew YHWH Yireh carries the idea of God's making provision when He sees the need. Notes on Genesis 22:11-14 from *New Spirit-Filled Life Bible,* Jack W. Hayford, ed. (Nashville, Thomas Nelson, 2002).

[107]Romans 12:6-8 is generally regarded as "the Father's creational gifts." An elaboration of such gifts is beyond the scope of this book. There are other resources that deal with the gifts of the Father, the Son, and the Holy Spirit in greater detail. A booklet entitled "Understanding and Discovering Spiritual Gifts" can be ordered through www.TableOfFriends.com.

[108]The subject of the baptism in the Holy Spirit is beyond the scope of this book. However, many books have been written on the subject that explain fully this Promise of the Father.

[109]For a full treatment of the Gifts of the Spirit, I recommend Kerry Wood, *The Gifts of the Spirit for a New Generation* (Zadok Publishing, 2015).

[110]When Paul uses the term "thorn in the flesh," he explains it as "a messenger of Satan to buffet me." The expression "thorn in the flesh" is used throughout Scripture to describe people – usually enemy armies. See Numbers 33:55; Joshua 23:13; Judges 2:3; Ezekiel 2:6; or Ezekiel 28:24. It is never used to refer to a bodily affliction.

[111]Horst Robert Balz and Gerhard Schneider, *Exegetical Dictionary of the New Testament, Vol. 3* (Grand Rapids: Eerdmans, 1990), 457.

[112]F.F. Bosworth, Christ the Healer (Grand Rapids: Fleming H. Revell, 2004), 31-3.

[113]Ken Blue, *Authority to Heal* (Downers Grove: IVP Books, 1987), 71-73.

[114]Ibid., 40.

[115]Dallas Willard, *The Spirit of the Disciplines: Understanding How God Changes Lives* (San Francisco: HarperCollins, 1991), 208.

[116]We can assume that the Pharisees and other devout Jews were all well versed in Scripture; but they did not carry the identity of sonship.

[117]Space doesn't allow for a detailed description of spiritual disciplines. Great books have been written on that subject. I recommend the following: Willard, *The Spirit of the Disciplines: Understanding How God Changes Lives* (San Francisco: HarperCollins, 1991). Jack W. Hayford, *Living the Spirit-Formed Life* (Ventura, CA: Regal Books, 2001).

[118]Paul Tillich, T*he Courage to Be, 3rd ed.* (Yale University Press, 2014).

[119]Skye Jethani, *With: Reimagining the Way You Relate to God* (Nashville: Thomas Nelson, 2011), 151-2.

[120]This is the definition of the word *pleroma, Strong's* #4138. Jack W. Hayford, ed. *The Hayford Bible Handbook.* (Nashville, Thomas Nelson, 1995), 619.

[121]Parsing Information: *Strong's* G4137—*plēroō, Blue Letter Bible* (November 18, 2017), https://www.blueletterbible.org/nkjv /eph/5/18/t_conc_1102018

[122]Manning, *A Stranger to Self-Hatred,* 103.

Bibliography

à Kempis, Thomas. *The Imitation of Christ*. London: Penguin Books, 1952.

Anderson, Ray S. The Soul of Ministry. Louisville: Westminster John Knox Press, 1997.

Balz, Horst Robert and Gerhard Schneider. *Exegetical Dictionary of the New Testament*, Vol. 3. Grand Rapids: Eerdmans, 1990.

Barth, Karl. *The Humanity of God*, trans. John Newton Thomas and Thomas Wieser. London: Collins Clear-type Press, 1961.

Belliotti, Raymond Angelo. *Roman Philosophy and the Good Life*. Plymouth, UK: Lexington Books, 2009.

Berkhof, L. *Teología Sistemática*, trans. Felipe Delgado Cortés. Grand Rapids, Eerdmans, 1979.

Blue, Ken. *Authority to Heal*. Downers Grove: IVP Books, 1987.

Bosworth, F.F. *Christ the Healer*. Grand Rapids: Fleming H. Revell, 2004.

Fee, Gordon D. *GOD's Empowering Presence: The Holy Spirit in the Letters of Paul*. Peabody, MA: Hendrickson, 1994.

Folsom, Martin. "Relational Theology." Lecture presented in Relational Theology D.Min. seminar, Van Nuys, California, October 17-19, 2013. The King's University, Van Nuys, CA.

Folsom, Martin and Wesley M. Pinkham. *Relational Theology: A Primer*, [CD-ROM]. Lookout Mountain, TN: Journeys to the Heart, 2002.

Forster, Roger T. and V. Paul Marston, *God's Strategy in Human History*. Wheaton: Tyndale House Publishers, Inc., 1974.

Grenz, Stanley J. *Theology for the Community of God*. Grand Rapids: Eerdmans, 1994.

Gunton, Colin E. *The Promise of Trinitarian Theology*, 2nd ed. (New York: T&T Clark Ltd., 1997.

———. *The One, the Three and the Many: God, Creation and the Culture of Modernity*. Cambridge: Cambridge University Press, 1998.

Hayford, Jack W. *Living the Spirit-Formed Life*. Ventura, CA: Regal Books, 2001.

———. *Pastors of Promise: Pointing to Character and Hope as the Keys to Fruitful Shepherding*. Ventura: Regal Books, 1997.

Hayford, Jack W., ed. *The Hayford Bible Handbook*. Nashville, Thomas Nelson, 1995.

———. *New Spirit-Filled Life Bible*. Nashville, Thomas Nelson, 2002.

Huntzinger, Jon. "Characteristics of the Holy Spirit." Lectures, presented in Biblical Resources for Ministry D.Min. seminar, Van Nuys, California, June 12, 2012. The King's University, Van Nuys, CA.

Jeremias, Joachim. *The Central Message of the New Testament*. London: SCM Press, 1965.

Jethani, Skye. *With: Reimagining the Way You Relate to God*. Nashville: Thomas Nelson, 2011.

Kohls, L. Robert. "The Values Americans Live By," Claremont McKenna College. January 10, 2017. http://www1.cmc.edu/pages/faculty/alee/extra/American_values.html

Kruger, C. Baxter. *The Great Dance: The Christian Vision Revisited*. Vancouver: Regent College Publishing, 2000.

Ladd, George Eldon. *The Gospel of the Kingdom: Popular Expositions on the Kingdom of God*. Grand Rapids: Eerdmans, 1983.

———. *The Gospel of the Kingdom: Scriptural Studies in the Kingdom of God*. Grand Rapids: Eerdmans, 1997.

Macmurray, John. *Freedom in the Modern World: Broadcast Talks on Modern Problems*. London: Faber & Faber Limited, 1934.

———. *Persons in Relation*. Atlantic Highlands, NJ: Humanities Press, 1979.

Manning, Brennan. *A Stranger to Self-Hatred: A Glimpse of Jesus*. Denville, NJ: Dimension Books, 1982.

———. *The Ragamuffin Gospel: Embracing the Unconditional Love of God*. Sisters, OR: Multnomah Books, 1990.

McFadyen, Alistair I. *The Call to Personhood: A Christian Theory of the Individual in Social Relationships*. Cambridge: Cambridge University Press, 1990.

Moltmann, Jürgen. *The Spirit of Life: A Universal Affirmation*. Minneapolis: Fortress, 1992.

Nouwen, Henri J. M. A *Cry for Mercy*. Garden City, NY: Doubleday & Co., 1981.

Pinkham, Wesley M. *Identity Formation: The Journey toward Personhood*. Lookout Mountain: Journeys to the Heart, Inc., 2003.

Oord, Thomas J. *The Uncontrolling Love of God: An Open and Relational Account of Providence*. Downers Grove: IVP Academic, 2015.

Pinkham, Wesley M. and Chris Waters. Creative Conflict Management. Lookout Mountain: Journeys to the Heart, Inc., 2001.

Pinnock, Clark H. *Flame of Love: A Theology of the Holy Spirit*. Downers Grove: IVP Academic, 1996.

Polo-Wood, Chiqui. *Lessons Learned in the Battle: How to Live in Victory,*

No Matter What. Bedford, TX: Burkhart Books, 2015.

Schaeffer, Francis A. *The God Who Is There.* Downers Grove: Inter-Varsity Press, 1968.

Torrance, James B. *Worship, Community and the Triune God of Grace.* Downers Grove: IVP Academic, 1996.

Torrance, Thomas F. *The Christian Doctrine of God: One Being, Three Persons.* Edinburgh: T & T Clark, 1996.

———. *The Ground and Grammar of Theology.* Charlottesville: University Press of Virginia, 1980.

Tozer, A.W. *The Knowledge of the Holy: The Attributes of God: Their Meaning in the Christian Life.* New York: Harper Collins, 1961.

Twelftree, Graham H. *People of the Spirit: Exploring Luke's View of the Church.* Grand Rapids: Baker Academic, 2009.

Unger, Merrill F. *Unger's Bible Dictionary.* Chicago: Moody Press, 1979.

Waters, Chris and Wess Pinkham. *Finding Closure to the Pains from the Past.* Lookout Mountain: Journeys to the Heart, Inc., 2006.

Willard, Dallas. T*he Divine Conspiracy: Rediscovering Our Hidden Life in God.* San Francisco: HarperCollins, 1997.

———. *The Spirit of the Disciplines: Understanding How God Changes Lives.* San Francisco: HarperCollins, 1991.

Williams, Rowan. "Archbishop's address to the Synod of Bishops in Rome, Wednesday 10th October 2012." Dr. Rowan Williams, 104th Archbishop of Canterbury. Published 2012. Accessed July 14, 2017. http://rowanwilliams.archbishopofcanterbury .org/articles/php/2645/archbishops-address-to-the-synod-of-bishops-in-rome

Wood, Ana. "Relational Discipleship: The Formation of Persons in Relationship as the Foundation for Discipleship." D.Min. proj., The King's University, 2014.

Wood, Kerry. *The Gifts of the Spirit for a New Generation.* Zadok Publishing, 2015.

———. *The Abba Factor.* Bedford, TX: Burkhart Books, 2018.

———. *The Abba Formation.* Bedford, TX: Burkhart Books, 2018.

———. "Participating in the Ministry of Christ: The Contribution of Trinitarian Theology to an Understanding of the Nature of Pastoral Leadership." D.Min. proj., The King's University, 2012.

Wright, N.T. *Following Jesus: Biblical Reflections on Discipleship.* Grand Rapids: Eerdmans, 1995.

Yeomans, Lillian B. *His Healing Power: Four Classic Books on Healing, Complete in One Volume.* Tulsa, OK: Harrison House, 2006.

About the Author

Ana Isabel "Chiqui" Polo-Wood was raised in Bogotá, Colombia, in the home of Pedro Polo and Alicia Fonnegra. She came to know Jesus as Lord and savior at age 15, and over the last 30 years has served in many areas of ministry including Teacher, Mentor, Associate Pastor, and Director of Adult Education. God has given her many opportunities to travel to several other nations to preach, train teachers and help local Church leaders start Leadership Institutes for their congregations. She lives in Texas with her husband, Kerry. They love ministering together both locally and abroad.

Chiqui is passionate for the Word and the presence of God, and continually amazed at the realization that the Triune God has chosen to partner with humanity to establish His Kingdom on earth. Her desire and goal in ministry is to see the Body of Christ fully equipped to live in the fullness of life that the Father has prepared for His children.

Chiqui earned her Master of Divinity (Outstanding Scholar) and Doctor of Ministry from The King's University, Los Angeles, California in 2011 and 2014 respectively. In addition, she is the author of the book, *Lessons Learned in the Battle*.

www.ChiquiPoloWood.com
&
www.tableoffriends.com

Check out the other two books in the trilogy:

THE ABBA FACTOR:
See yourself through the Father's eyes and understand the progression from an orphan spirit to the spirit of sonship.

THE ABBA FORMATION:
Do you want to go deeper? Learn to partner with Holy Spirit who searches the Father's heart and discloses His purposes to you through spiritual words.